BASIC TRAINING OF THE YOUNG HORSE

Ahlerich who Reiner Klimke trained to be the 1982 World Dressage Champion, the 1984 Individual and Team Olympic Gold Medallist and 1985 European Champion. The facial expression of the horse shows a personality full of life and intelligence.

Basic Training of the Young Horse

Reiner Klimke
Translated by Sigrid Young. Edited by Jane Kidd

THE LYONS PRESS

Foreword

For years experts have written about the art of riding including the education of the young horse. This makes it difficult to find something new to say but Dr Reiner Klimke has been able to achieve this because he is one of the world's most successful riders and is able to combine to an extraordinary degree theoretical knowledge with his own riding ability. As well as this, he has spent more than 25 years educating young horses, first at the Reitverein Wesbevern and later at the Westfalen Reit-und Fahr-Schule.

In both Eventing and Dressage no other rider has had such great success with horses schooled by himself and this included at the German, European and World Championships, as well as the Olympics.

Klimke's advice and thoughts are based on the valuable experience he has gained in these competitions. His successes alone qualify him to give his opinions about the correct way to educate a young horse. The comments in this book are clear and easily understood so that they are helpful to young riders as well as the experienced breeders and trainers who wish to train their young horses from the very beginning. All his advice is based on methods which he himself has proved to be successful.

It must be pointed out that this book is not aimed exclusively at the education of a dressage horse. Klimke makes it clear that a sound basic training helps all horses to develop their natural ability, regardless of whether the horse will be used for jumping, eventing or dressage.

The author not only gives help and advice about the basic training for riding but also discusses his experiences so there is much to read that has not been written before. All in all the book is an excellent guide to the education of young horses based on sound, practical and theoretical knowledge.

Dr Reiner Klimke has already achieved renown as the author of *Horse Trials* and *Cavalletti*. Both books showed the way to the correct education of the horse based on the classic principles. This new book, *Basic Training of the Young Horse* has the same aim.

PAUL STECKEN
Westfalian Riding and Driving School

Contents

Editor's Note

Translations from the German are not easy as there are many words which have no direct translation. The German equestrian vocabulary is much fuller than the British. Therefore, in order to ensure that the fullest possible understanding of Dr Klimke's training methods are obtained in English I thought it best to leave some very important German words. Hence words like *losgelassen* (which is usually translated as loose and supple), *takt* (rhythm), *schwung* (impulsion) and *durchlassigkeit* (obedience) are left. A full explanation of what they mean is given when they are first used and the reader will discover that this is much more than the equivalents they are given in English.

I had great assistance in my work as editor. Sigrid Young did the translation and, having been born and brought up in Germany, ridden international dressage for Britain and judged up to a high level, she has excellent credentials. Dr Klimke himself spent much time explaining in greater detail some aspects of the training (for example, the training scale) which the Germans take for granted but the British know little about. Hence this English translation has some additions to the German book. Finally Claudia Koch, fluent in German provided more expertise to clarify the difficult ideas to express in English.

I know I have been inspired and educated by this book – I hope others will be too.

JANE KIDD

1 The Goals of Basic Training

We live in a time of change. Modern technology has simplified and speeded up many things, so that what used to take years is now achieved in a fraction of the time. Speed plays a large part in our lives and also, unfortunately, in our connection with horses. Nowadays 3-year-old horses are offered at auction sales as top potential dressage, jumpers or event horses in the belief that these horses, which have only just been backed, will reach the top in these disciplines.

To the experienced horseman this is sheer nonsense. He knows that patience is needed on the long route which brings a horse from basic training to the top of a discipline. But how many lovers of horses have enough knowledge of horsemanship? Since the Second World War, equestrian sports have attracted more and more followers not only from the country but from the towns as well. A new generation of keen riders has emerged. They have not grown up with horses. They like to spend their free time riding as a means of bringing them closer to nature. Often a horse is regarded merely as a piece of sports equipment. Hence, knowledge of training and horsemanship has generally diminished.

It is easy to understand why the not so knowledgeable rider believes the auctioneer's sales talk. The results are quite noticeable at horse shows. How often one sees horses jumping with their heads pulled into their chests when they have not learned to balance themselves in the three paces and yet are expected to jump in classes L and M (equivalent British grade B and C classes). How many dressage horses have difficulties getting over an obedience jump, have never seen cavalletti or been allowed to enjoy a peaceful hack with their rider? (In Germany in novice dressage tests competitors are required to jump a small obstacle (obedience jump) upon completing the test.) I believe that much leg trouble in horses is due to their starting specialised training too early.

Basic training has the aim of preparing the unbacked or just backed horse with systematic graduated training, thereby laying a sound foundation for future specialisation. This early work must not be restricted to a specialised channel, as the aim is to develop the natural capabilities of the whole horse. What we want to achieve is for the horse to move as freely with as without a rider. If the horse moves and carries itself in such a way then a basis is established for future development. The aim of the basic training of the young horse is achieved when:

(a) the horse accepts all demands connected with its future use (i.e. in the stable, indoor school, strange surroundings, dressage arena, show jumping courses etc.);

(b) the horse accepts the aids of the rider and learns to follow them (especially seat, leg and rein aids);

(c) the horse gains enough confidence, strength, and endurance to go through a novice test without too many mistakes; a small jumping course obediently; and cross-country course at a prescribed speed with safety.

When these basic demands have been met, it will transpire to which of the various disciplines the horse is suited or that the horse has reached its limit. We must be fair to the horse and only try to bring out what is in him. We must follow the principle that we can only develop what nature gave to the horse.

Just as not everyone can be a top athlete nor can every horse reach the top of its discipline. As the majority of riders are satisfied at being able to put up a good show in novice classes this has advantages. We should realise that this achievement can bring happiness and satisfaction and too many riders set their sights too high for themselves and their horses and thereby lose the happiness riding can bring them. They do damage not only to themselves but also to their horses who are asked to do things beyond their capabilities.

Few problems should arise in the basic training. If they do it is evident that a horse, which has difficulties in getting to novice level, is not going to be suitable as a competition horse.

The basic training gives useful hints to the experienced rider about the future capabilities of his young horse. I have made dressage horses out of several horses that were deemed to be jumpers. It turned out that they were overcautious and therefore jumped very big over small obstacles but lacked the courage when it came to the bigger fences.

On the other hand I have had horses that had a so-called talent for dressage but developed a real talent for jumping when they were put on the bit and could therefore utilise their strength. The all-round education of the young horse is important whether it is going to be a hack or a competition horse. Through the careful development of the muscles and by well thought out gymnastic exercises the horse will stay sound and healthy longer and will be more able to cope with its specialised discipline.

2 The Handling and Education of the Young Horse

Normally we riders buy horses that are three or four years old. Only a few of us have the chance to educate the very young horse ourselves. In spite of this, one should have a cursory knowledge of how a young horse should be treated and educated until it is first mounted. I will, however, only go into the handling and education of the horse and not the feeding.

One can tell by the behaviour of the young horse how it has been handled.

A 3-year-old that has been handled since birth and had contact with people is of course much easier to teach than a youngster which has never worn a head collar and has been brought up in a remote field with little human contact. However, I would personally prefer to take on such a youngster. Of course they are often more nervous and need greater care at the beginning. On the other hand they are often more attached to their trainer once he has gained their confidence.

Problems are apt to develop in the training of a young horse that has been coddled, and sometimes even made flabby, and in others which have had bad experiences. The spoiled horse can be re-adjusted with care by the trainer, but it should be remembered that it is not advisable to humanise a horse. Nor should one compare the horse with the much loved house dog which is more able to imitate human behaviour.

It is of course much harder to win the confidence of a young horse which has had bad experiences in its relationship with people. These horses are usually the ones that give one the most work during the basic training. One first has to establish what were the bad things that the youngster had experienced in its relationship with people. Biting, shying, kicking, tense paces are often the result of bad treatment.

Education starts with the foal

By careful handling and treatment of the young horse, a breeder creates in it a confidence which will be needed for the work the rider will eventually ask the horse to do.

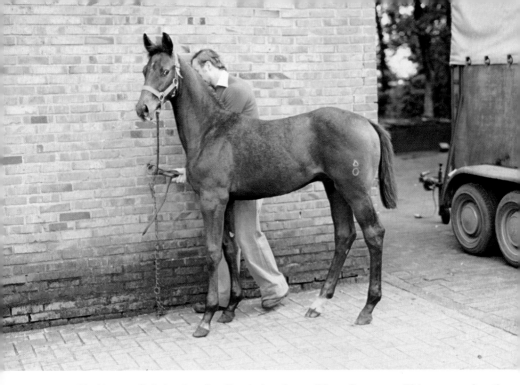

Foal in a well-fitting head-collar tied to the wall by a firm rope. This soon makes the foal realise that it is useless to try and get free

Education starts with the putting on of the halter. The aim is to make it clear to the foal that it only punishes itself by resisting. To prove this point to the foal, a well fitting head collar should be put on and be attached by a chain to a ring in the wall – thereby making any resistance useless.

As trainers we must act quickly and decisively. If we hesitate and show indecision, we ask for resistance. The foal must respect its trainer and realise he is of a higher intelligence. This has nothing to do with roughness. Respect and confidence are not opposites but complement each other and are merely ingredients of a successful education. We gain the confidence of the horse if we let it relax as soon as it has obeyed our wishes. A short word of praise is enough as too much fuss encourages the foal to be playful and this results in kicks and nips.

Foals are nosey. They want to investigate things, to lick them and chew them whether it be the halter, the rope, mother's mane and tail or the arm of their groom. If one encourages the foal and plays with it one must not be surprised to get some bruises. Unfortunately if a foal does bite it is often interpreted as nastiness. Then punishment follows and, quite often, thereby plants the seeds of bad temper, or of timidity and nervousness in the horse. The experienced breeder does not go in for such games. He watches the foal from a distance and handles it only in the short period of its education.

Having got the head collar on the foal, one must now get it accepted. Getting the foal used to the head collar can begin in the first few weeks of its life. If one deals with a lively foal the best time to start is when it is tired, has been fed and lies quietly in its box. Go to the left of the foal, put your right arm over its head and ease the halter over the foal's head with both hands. Under no circumstances stand in front of the foal and try to put the halter over its head as the foal will get frightened and pull away. After putting on the halter talk to the foal and pat it on the neck as a reward. The halter should be removed after a short time. If this exercise is repeated for a few days, the foal will soon accept it and take it for granted. We can then continue with the foal's education, teaching it to stand tied up so that we can groom it later on.

When tying up the foal for the first time, it is especially important to ensure that the halter and rope fit well and are strong. The foal will probably try to free itself when it feels the restriction of the rope. That is why it is so important that nothing gives way, so that the foal soon realises that it is useless to resist. This exercise should be concluded with praise and repeated on the following days. If possible tie up the foal at the same spot each day, preferably in the stable near the feed bowl. Let the foal get used to being tied up there, before it is tied up outside in the yard. One should also stay in the vicinity of the mare's stable so that she does not lose sight of her foal and become restless.

Putting the halter on the foal

Next we practice grooming and picking up feet. Foals like the feel of the brush or curry comb through their tangled coat. They usually try to nibble the groom, as if to say "thank you". To escape this attention gently turn your head away or issue a short reprimand "none of that". In a short time the foal will realise that this kind of loving attention is not welcome.

The foal soon learns to pick up its feet when asked. One should start by lifting the leg which is carrying least weight and not too high so that the foal does not lose balance. It makes no difference whether the front or hind legs are picked up first. As one lifts the leg give the short command "give". The foal will get used to this and in future will lift its leg when only a slight tap on its leg and the command are given.

The most difficult part of the education of the foal is to get it used to being led with the halter and rope. This needs two people, one for the mare and one for the foal. If the mare is led in front the foal will follow willingly, although there will come the moment when the foal feels the rope and resists. The trainer will have to show considerable understanding. If he pulls, he will make the foal stubborn and inclined to fight him, which is not only unnecessary but dangerous as the foal will develop strength which is greater than that of the trainer. I remember one occasion when a handler tried to force a foal along when it was stubborn and resisted him but the foal panicked and dragged the handler along until he had to let go. The best advice under these circumstances is to give in, step beside the foal and keep contact with it on the halter.

Mare with foal at foot. In Germany the foal is tied to the mare when shown in Mare and Foal classes

The trainer must speak firmly to the foal, perhaps even pat its neck to encourage it to move on. The handler of the mare should walk on with her as the further the mare moves away the more likely it is that the foal will follow. The trainer should not look back or at the foal as experience shows that this makes the foal even more stubborn.

Experienced trainers are satisfied when the foal accepts being brushed, lifts its feet and can be led by its halter. More should not be asked of the youngster.

The training of the riding horse is lengthy and difficult. We should give the young horse a chance to grow up as close to nature as possible in its first and second year. It should be turned out in a field as much as possible. The important factors are good feeding, knowledgeable handling and care of its feet.

At what age is a horse ready to be ridden?

There are trainers that start loose jumping yearlings and 2-year-olds. There are also trainers that lunge these youngsters. I am not in agreement with either of these methods. Anyone who knows anything about the growth of a young horse knows that it is damaging to the warmblood's health to have work of any sort in its first and second year, especially as yearlings and 2-year-olds grow in different phases. They grow at times more quickly in front and at other times behind which make it very difficult for them to be balanced. I realise that there is a tendency for breeders to start their young stock too early in order to produce them at auction as ridden 3-year-olds. Although racehorses run their first races as 2-year-olds and as 3-year-olds run in the Derby, I believe that the experienced trainer of riding horses will not start work with his charge until the growth of the joints, bones and tendons is well advanced.

No warmblood horse should be ridden until it is three to three and a half years old. I personally do not ride a horse under three years. I am guided by the following consideration – horses that are born early in the year therefore develop earlier. These I start in April for four to six weeks by getting them used to their new surroundings, the riding school, snaffle, lunge and saddle. Perhaps I will ride them a little, before turning them out to enjoy the summer. I start regular work under the rider in the autumn.

Horses that are born in the second half of the year are lunged but not ridden before being turned out for the summer. I feel it would be a pity to ride them as they are not sufficiently developed. I only start riding them in the autumn at the end of their third year.

It is my experience that if I stick to these guidelines the horses' education progresses more quickly and with fewer problems. None of my successful horses have been shown as 3-year-olds. I bought "Winzerin", my three-day event horse at the 1960 Rome Olympics, as a 4-year-old in 1956. She had just been backed. "Arcadius" came to me as a 4-year-old just backed. I only started working him seriously at the end of his fourth year and when he was   17 a 7-year-old in 1962 we won the European Championships in Rotterdam. I bought "Fabiola" as a 2½-year-old, started riding her a year later, and won the Dressage Derby with her in Hamburg when she was a 6-year-old. I bought "Ahlerich" as a 4-year-old at the Westphalian Auction at Munster. I hardly rode him as a 4-year-old and only took him to one show. He won 10 medium and advanced classes as a 6-year-old and as a 7-year-old 9 Grand Prix classes.

I am convinced that had I started these horses earlier I would not have been so successful. One must have the patience to wait until the horse is physically and mentally ready for the work demanded of it. In my opinion one's goal is achieved sooner and provided no accident occurs the horse will stay sound longer.

The transition from field to stable

It is difficult to know what a horse has been doing when it first comes to you as a 3-year-old for further education. One should make a point of finding out under what conditions it has grown up and what it has already been asked to do, though one will seldom hear the full truth as usually everyone thinks the horse is perfect. A certain amount of scepticism is therefore necessary.

Even with the best of information about a horse I like to form my own judgement and treat it with great caution. I always make an effort to be there when the young horse arrives. I watch carefully how it unloads and, if possible, let it walk and trot up before it goes into its new box. I make sure that everything is quiet and keep inquisitive spectators away to enable the horse to adjust to its completely new surroundings.

The horse's first impression of its new surroundings is very important and influences future behaviour. I make certain there is a nice clean bed and that the groom keeps visitors away. The horse will be occupied with getting used to its new home and this is the time when it will get to know its groom. As the trainer of the horse I therefore keep away for the first four or five days.

If at all possible in the first few weeks I like to have just one groom looking after the young horse as the different behaviour of various people can affect its nervous system. To be handled by too many other people can make a young horse suspicious and nervous of the groom and trainer.

As a rule the young horse comes in from grass to be schooled and attention has therefore to be given to its feeding routine. Horses that come directly off grass at first should be given approximately 3 to 5 lb oats. To balance this, they should have more hay, approximately 12 to 15 lb and sufficient bran. The box should be freshened up with new straw about twice a day. A good change is to give some carrots (1 to 2 lb) about two or three times a week.

An open mind should be kept about feeding and those new products discussed and advertised in the equestrian magazines and trade publications. Riders, and even more so grooms, are inclined to be rather conservative with feeding routines. They tend to swear by the conventional use of oats, hay and straw and are critical of any new feed products, but this is better than making a guinea pig of the horse using any new feed that comes on the market. It is a good idea to ask the advice of a vet when changing a horse's diet, as well as which additives (e.g. vitamins, licks, etc.) are most suitable to put in the basic feed.

Exercise is most important when the horse comes in from grass to work. We must not forget that the horse has a very strongly developed motive power and is the most highly developed mammal. Dr Wilhelm Blendinger points out in his book *Psychologic und Veshaltunigsweise des Pfendes* that the horse nowadays suffers from too little exercise rather than too much. It is not possible to give the stabled young horse as much exercise as it had when it was out at grass, and indeed this is not necessary. We should make sure, however, that the young horse, starting from two days after its arrival, has at least one full hour's exercise. It is best to divide this into a 30 minute session in the morning and afternoon.

We can happily leave this exercising to the groom and just watch. This will make it much easier for the young horse to get used to its groom and gain confidence in him. It is best to let the horse free in the school for about 15 minutes to let it get rid of some of its excess energy. In the afternoon walking the horse round the stable yard and surroundings will help it get used to them. The horse may not be accustomed to being groomed so this is the time to teach it to have its feet cleaned out, to be brushed and have its sheath and backside cleaned. A firm but quiet approach to this is most important in the same way as we have discussed in handling foals. The experienced groom talks quietly to his horse. He uses short words of command, such as "stand", "give", "Good". A lot of talk just confuses the horse and it would not understand.

Many horses suffer from too little exercise. Allowing them total freedom in the school for 15 minutes per day helps in the transition from grass to stable and training

Observing the horse

Generally we should be careful, when handling horses, not to treat them as if they were human beings. To feed them sugar and tit-bits at any old time is asking for trouble. Instead of excessive coddling we should watch our horse carefully and then, by drawing our own conclusions as to its mental condition, treat it accordingly. The objects of this scrutiny should be the eyes, ears, facial expression, tail, voice, snorting, sweating and paces.

EYES   We can learn a great deal about the character and temperament of the horse from its eye. A quiet, clear eye with a gentle expression is the sign of a kind character. Horses with eyes that are small and have unkind expression are often bad tempered. When a lot of white shows in the eyes it is said that the horse is full of energy and therefore sometimes uncontrollable.

If the eye is restless it shows that the horse is anxious. This is not uncommon when the horse is changing stables and shows that it has not yet gained full confidence in its groom and become used to its new surroundings. If this expression continues in spite of kind handling it is worrying as the anxious eye may mean pain. In such cases a vet should be consulted.

EARS   The mood of the horse can be deducted from the movement of its ears. Pricked ears signal a good mood. Ears that are pricked but turned slightly back mean great attention is being paid. Ears flat back are a sign of discomfort and when we notice this we have to watch out as such a horse is on the defensive and could suddenly kick or bite. We must speak to it sharply and firmly.

FACIAL EXPRESSION   When first watching a horses' face it is not so easy to understand its expressions. These are very varied and include the movement of the lips and nostrils and the expression in the eye. To be able to understand them is one of the most satisfying experiences when dealing with horses.

TAIL   A quietly swinging tail tells us of a happy and relaxed horse. A tail carried very high or tightly between its legs denotes tension or excitement and a few short bucks often follow for fun. When it has got rid of some of its excess energy the tail carriage returns to normal. Horses that often swish their tails are usually ticklish. One should not ride them too soon with spurs and one should adjust to their super sensitivity.

Horses that have been racing or young horses that have had excessive work often start swishing their tails. This is a warning sign of tiredness.

VOICE   Horses handle their voices in different ways. Some horses are hardly ever heard using their voices loudly. There are others that greet their fellow horses with a loud whinny. My Olympic horse "Dux", for example, always drew attention to itself with a friendly whinny when arriving at new surroundings. A young horse often whinnies when its stable companions go off and leave it behind. It is not difficult to teach a horse to whinny as a greeting as all that is necessary is to take a snack when going to see it. Often horses give a deep whinny when food is on its way.

Should a horse groan, scream or moan one can be sure that it is in pain. Help should be called for immediately.

Short little snorts and squeals are the noises which a horse uses to show its ticklishness. They are often heard when two horses sniff each other. This is usually followed by a friendly bite or kick. Mares in season usually make these noises.

SNORTING Snorting is a sign of contentment. The horse shows that it is relaxed and without tension. One has to differentiate between this and a noise more like snoring when breathing in and quickly repeated snorts when exhaling. This is sometimes heard in a galloping thoroughbred which is excited and hears a frightening noise in the distance, or something unknown and threatening coming near. Laymen often mistake this with a horse which has a wind problem and makes a noise (gone in the wind).

SWEATING It is natural for the horse to sweat when it has been working. It shows us the degree of effort made and is a guide as to how much or little to ask of the horse.

When in pain, for instance during an attack of colic, a sudden breaking out in sweat is usual. However, young horses can break out in sweat due to excitement when they might shake and their hearts can be felt beating.

PACES The horse's paces are the key to its capabilities. This is why special attention has to be paid to them.

It is quite normal for a young horse, when it first leaves the stable, to move rather stiffly and tensely. When at grass it was able to move around all the day, now it has to adjust to remaining in a restricted space for a long time. It has to get over this loss of freedom of movement. In a little while it will settle down and then it is possible to study its movement. For example, quite accurate conclusions can be drawn about the horse's future canter when watching to see whether it is balanced or not when negotiating the short side of the school. The way it trots points the way to its future capabilities.

A whole book could be written about the conclusions that can be drawn from watching free moving horses and the help this gives to their education. Watching the horse too is a valuable addition to what the rider feels under the saddle.

Getting used to saddle and bit

So far the young horse has only encountered the head collar and rope. Now   21

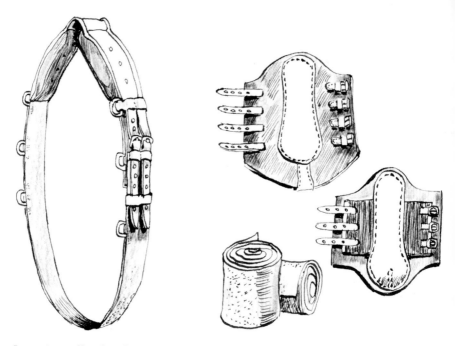

Lungeing roller, bandages and boots

we have to get it used to all the other equipment before we can continue with the training. The person to do this is the groom who has been looking after the youngster and who has gained its confidence.

With difficult horses the groom can use a few special tricks. New, threatening articles can be brought into the box at the same time as the feed. The horse is tied up and allowed to feed in the normal way. At that stage the groom puts on, for example, the roller and boots. Similarly, boots and bandages can also be put on after the horse is groomed in the yard. It is advisable to be careful when putting on the rug and roller for the first time as the horse might throw itself down, however carefully the rugging-up is done.

I use both boots and bandages on young horses. Boots are perhaps better and easier to clean; bandages have to be washed more often. As my horses are not shod during their first winter in work it is immaterial whether I use boots or bandages to protect them against over-reaching or developing splints. When horses are shod it may be better to use leather boots, although there is no strict rule about this.

There are trainers who hold the opinion, with good reason, that young horses should go without boots or bandages in order to prevent them becoming soft. They believe they should correct themselves when they knock their legs. The adherents of this method also believe that too much early support of the front tendons stops them from developing and strengthening as nature intended.

I do not want to argue with this point of view as I too am of the opinion that one should not tamper with nature; but I do want to prevent the formation of splints and therefore always lunge or ride my horses with bandages or boots. Only the fore legs are protected; I leave the hind legs alone. The danger of developing splints through knocking of hinds is so slight that I prefer the natural method. I try as much as possible not to soften the horses too much. If the horse is a straight mover the danger of knocking is reduced.

CORRECTLY ADJUSTED SNAFFLE It is not possible to combine the putting on of the bridle with feeding. In my experience it is best to do it after feeding.

Since starting to ride young horses I have always used a snaffle with a drop noseband and I intend to carry on in this way in the future although one sees more and more young horses with special bits and bridles.

The drop noseband is used to keep the horses' mouth closed and to stop it avoiding the bit by moving its lower jaw. The cavesson noseband is similar to the one used on a double bridle and acts above the bit. The grackle puts more pressure on the nose.

It is quite obvious that only a properly adjusted bit will encourage a horse to accept it and thus avoid future difficulties in the mouth. Please pay special attention to this. At this point I would also like to point out that too often the noseband is fastened too tightly.

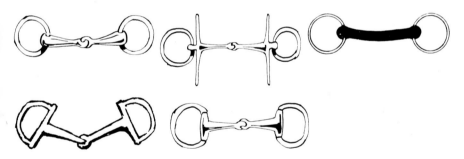

The most common and German LPO approved permitted bits (*top line, from left to right*): Snaffle metal or rubber; Snaffle with cheeks; Straight rubber snaffle (*bottom*) "D" ended snaffle; Eggbut snaffle

Normally there should be enough room for two fingers in between the nose and the noseband. The horse does not feel too restricted then and yet cannot open its mouth. If I tighten the noseband too much I am asking for resistance in the mouth. Not only does it interfere with breathing, as the horse only breathes through its nose, but it feels altogether too restricted. It makes for a dead mouth and one can imagine the resistance against the hand this can create. Sometimes an occasional tightening of the noseband can   23

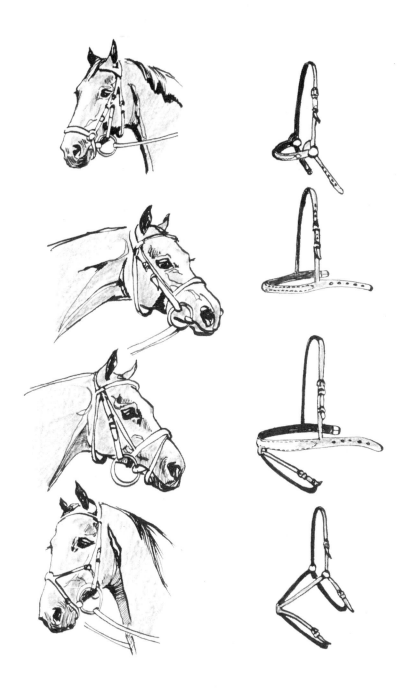

24   Snaffle: with drop noseband; cavesson noseband; flash; grackle

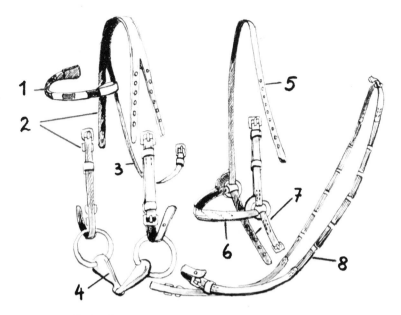

Parts of the snaffle bridle:
1. brow band   2. cheek pieces   3. throat lash   4. snaffle bit   5. head piece   6. nose band   7. chin strap   8. reins

Putting on the bridle. The reins are put over the horse's neck so that he cannot run away

prevent the horse from putting its tongue out, but it is not a permanent cure – especially if the horse becomes used to it and becomes so clever that the noseband has to be tightened more and more. I have cured this bad habit by going to the other extreme, loosening the noseband completely or by using a bridle without a drop for a while.

SADDLE   The horse should be stabled at least eight to ten days before a saddle is put on and then without stirrups or girth. Two or three days later the girth can be put on and during the following week gradually tightened.

Parts of the saddle: a) pommel b) seat c) panel d) saddleflap f) stirrup iron e) stirrup leather g) knee roll h) girthstrap i) sweat flaps k) gullet l) pommel n) stirrup bar m) cantle

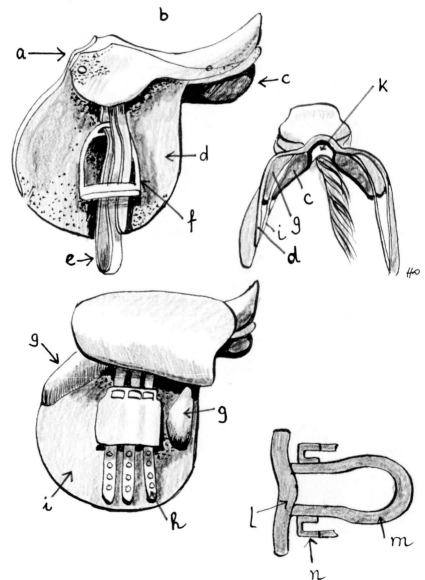

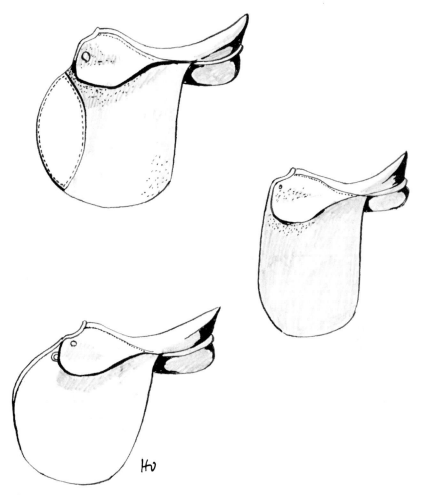

Saddles (*from top to bottom*): all-purpose saddle, Dressage saddle, jumping saddle

This stops the horse from blowing itself up. Other trainers do not put the saddle on until the horse has got used to being girthed up and lunged with a roller. This is a matter of personal preference. We have always put on the saddle at an early stage even if it is not used. Then we practice showing the horse in hand. Later, when the saddle is needed to show the horse under saddle the horse will remember it like an old friend, which has its advantages.

An all-purpose saddle is needed in the initial training of the young horse as the specialised saddles for jumping or dressage are a luxury at this stage. It is most important that the saddle fits the horse. Only if it fits properly and is well contoured can it help the rider to sit in the right position and be effective. It pays to ask for the advice of a professional and only buy the saddle after it has been tried on the horse without a numnah and fits perfectly.

Showing in-hand

When showing, the handler stops opposite the judge, steps forward to stand in front of the horse's head with his legs slightly apart. With the left hand he holds the right rein, and with the right hand the left rein at the height of the bit. The thumb should be on the snaffle rings and the reins in the right hand. The handler then makes sure that the horse is standing correctly and, if it is not, pulls the horse forward slightly or corrects it by pressing gently on its mouth.

When the horse is standing correctly the head should be lifted slightly to show off to the judge the neck and general conformation to the best advantage. The handler must ensure that the horse is standing on level ground – the clever ones even look for a place where the front legs are a bit higher than the hind legs so that the horse's body is pointing upwards. Such places can frequently be found when visiting a dealing yard. At official shows the organisers make sure these little tricks cannot be used by seeing to it that where the horses are shown the ground is level.

When showing, the handler steps back to the left of the horse's head and takes the reins into his right hand. The reins are separated by the middle and fore fingers and about the width of a hand from the snaffle. The right rein should be a little shorter than the left so that the horse's head is not pulled to the inside. The ends of the reins are looped through the right hand and held by the thumb.

Usually, a horse is shown in straight lines, up and down in front of the judges (turning to the right at the end of the line) first in walk then trot. When in-hand the handler walks or runs alongside the horse on its left about level with the horse's head. The right hand holds the reins at about shoulder

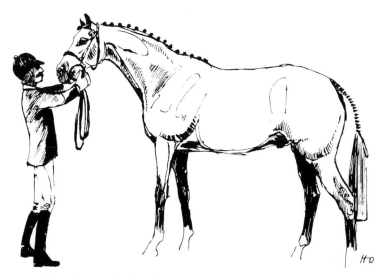

28   How to position a horse for showing

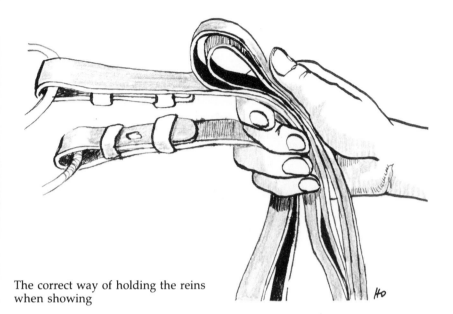

The correct way of holding the reins when showing

height and the left arm is relaxed at the handler's side. When trotting, the handler tries to keep in step with the horse.

These are the prescribed forms of showing in-hand. The above description makes it clear that we have to teach the young horse how to behave when shown. When practising I recommend taking a long whip. To begin with I stay next to the horse's left shoulder and hold the reins rather long, which makes it easier for me to obtain the horse's obedience. I am really taking it between the reins and whip so it is "on the aids".

First I walk along with the horse on a long rein as it was taught as a foal. I do not look at it when doing this and walk along in a "matter of fact" manner but positively so that it does not occur to the horse that this is something special. I then stop and say a quiet "halt". The young horse will quite likely take a few more steps but then halt because it is matching me. I give a slight tug on the reins but then quickly let go to counteract any possible resistance. A second command to "halt" may be necessary. When the horse stops I give it a pat with my right hand on the neck and pause for a few moments, looking at the horse all the time. I then look ahead, walk on, and say "walk on". The horse will follow me. If it should hesitate I give it a slight tap on the hocks with my whip.

This exercise: walk on – halt – walk on I repeat until it is fully established. This can take an entire week.

I only start this exercise after the horse has been turned loose in the school to get rid of some of its high spirits. Otherwise I may run into unnecessary problems. In spite of this the horse may get rather strong and want to run off – especially in trot, and this is where the handler has to act quickly. His reactions have to be a tenth of a second quicker than his horse's – he should give it one or two sharp jerks on the reins to make it clear to the horse that

In unison with the horse's strides. The showing of a young stallion. The Oldenburger "Uranius" by "Ultimo"

this means "stop! We do not go any further!". Under no circumstances must the rider pull on the reins. If he does this he risks the horse taking hold of the bit and pulling him along. A short but not too strong jerk will surprise the young horse and make it brake automatically.

Later, when obedience is more established I hold my left hand in front of the horse's face to give it confidence and quieten it in case it gets excited.

Lazy horses have to be encouraged by another person for showing in-hand. It is, however, very bad to crack a whip. Whilst this, and other noises, can of course create the impression of a fiery temperament and extravagant paces, on other occasions it may cause the horse to bolt upon hearing noises in the background. If this does happen, and one has used a whip previously, it should cause no surprise.

The training of a horse for showing is an important preparatory step in the education of the riding horse. Young horses that have gained confidence with people outside the stable yard are more mentally prepared to learn new things. Young horses that have had bad experiences when shown will remain suspicious for a long time afterwards. Handlers with rough and insensitive hands have many mouth problems on their conscience, and that is why young horses should only be shown by experienced people. I never let strangers show my horses; I do it myself or ask someone to whom they are used.

3 Lungeing and First Mounting

Now begins the real work of the trainer. Up until now it was acceptable for him to stay in the background and let the groom do the initial training, but now he has to take over – and become the most important person in the life of the young horse. The groom however does not become redundant. We still need him for much of the work, from lungeing to riding in.

Experts are very divided in their opinions as to whether it is advisable to lunge a horse before riding, and for how long. Herr Hans J. Kohler, who as the trainer of the young horses at Verden, has had more young horses through his hands since the Second World War than anyone else, does not believe in lungeing for any length of time. He is in favour of only a little lungeing and recommends that even after the first lungeing lesson, when the horse walks, the saddle should be put on and the rider lifted up. This method makes sense when looked at through the eye of the seller of the horse, especially if he is dealing, as at Verden, with top quality horses selected from a large number of candidates. When looked at through the eye of the trainer who has to develop the horse later on, a steadier progress would be appreciated.

Personally I do not like to tire horses by lungeing them for too long at one time, thereby taking too much out of them. In the first phase of the young horse's training I lunge it for 3 to 4 weeks before putting on a rider. I do this having taken into consideration the long way that lies ahead in the horse's training and the importance of its health and the freedom for growth and general development. As these are so important to me I am able to be patient.

Lungeing is still important as a basis for the training after the horse has been mounted. It is complimentary to and completes the work done by the trainer. Lungeing the horse before it is ridden is especially useful for horses with neck or back difficulties. Also when the horse has had one or two days rest lungeing for 15 to 20 minutes will take the edge off its energies.

Some days lungeing can be a substitute for riding. Perhaps one wants to examine from the ground what one has felt in the saddle or one wants to put the horse honestly on the bit by making it use its hind legs more actively. This will be discussed more thoroughly in later chapters when we talk about the actual training under the rider. I only want to say now – lungeing is as difficult as riding. The person who lunges needs considerable experience. If he does not do it correctly much damage can be done. Only an experienced person should be used and the programme discussed with him.

Lungeing

Work on the lunge prepares the horse for work under the saddle. The aids are learnt through the use of voice, whip and lunge rein. One should allow young horses a good long period on the lunge before they are ridden. The horse is not hampered by the weight of the rider to which it is not used and it will learn more easily to go on to the bit, relax and regain the rhythm of the paces in walk, trot and canter. A 3-year-old which is to be ridden in the spring should have been lunged for 4 weeks, and in the autumn at least 3 weeks.

LUNGEING EQUIPMENT Apart from the snaffle and boots or bandages we need the following: lunge roller, lunge rein, side reins, lunge cavesson, lunge whip.

The lunge roller, which is not padded, can be put over the saddle. If this is used it is only necessary to remove the roller before getting up on the horse which is practical. On either side of the roller are small rings to which the side reins can be attached at higher or lower levels.

The lunge cavesson nose band should be well padded and fastened firmly

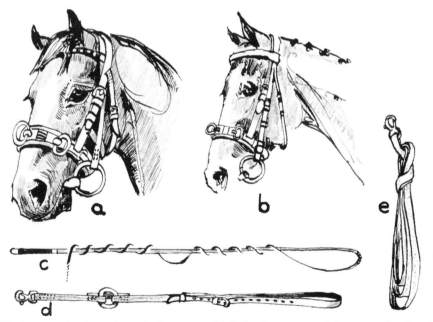

Equipment for lungeing: a) Cavesson   b) light Cavesson   c) lunge whip about
5–6 m long   d) side rein   e) lunge line 7–10 m long

Horse ready for lungeing: 4-year-old Westfalian gelding "Siamon" by Silvaner. The side reins are put on low to encourage him to lengthen his neck

so that it does not slip around. There are three rings on it. The lunge is put on the middle ring. The inside ring is used for horses that hang to the outside to stop the cavesson from being moved around.

The complete cavesson is quite complicated. It takes some time to put it on correctly, especially on a young horse.

First the snaffle bit is put on either with or without the bridle. After that the cavesson is put on. The throat lash is then tightened so that the cheek pieces do not rub and do not interfere with the horse's eyes.

The lighter cavesson is much easier to use. This is in the same shape as a snaffle bridle but with three rings on the noseband. I prefer this latter type of cavesson for young horses as the less tack it has on the freer it feels. Use of a cavesson ensures the aids are applied on the least tender parts of the horse's nose, and not on its mouth. The young horse should feel happy with the snaffle and not become frightened of its mouth if for various reasons it gets strong and has to be reprimanded.

If you are not able to use a cavesson, put the lunge rein on a chin strap attached to the snaffle ring and not on the inside ring otherwise the bit can be pulled sideways through the horse's mouth. A connecting strap can easily be made by running a spur strap through both the snaffle rings and fastening it. The lunge rein can also be attached through the inside snaffle ring and on to the noseband, or through one snaffle ring and then across the chin to the other, or through the inside snaffle ring over the head and onto the outer snaffle ring. The last has a much stronger effect than the others.

33

BTOAYH-C

The side reins are used as a substitute for the rider's hand and should help the horse to look for and take the bit with confidence. A correctly prepared horse is one that when walking on the lunge the side reins are long enough not to interfere with the horse's movement. The inside rein is, according to the size of the circle, 2 to 3 holes shorter than the outside rein.

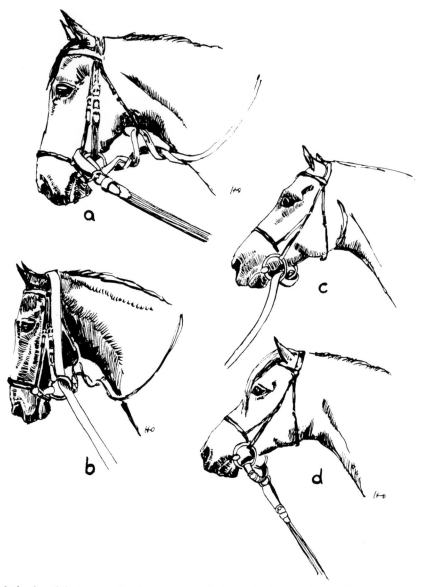

Methods of fastening the lunge rein: a) through the inside snaffle ring to the noseband;   b) through the inside snaffle ring over the head to the outside snaffle ring;   c) through the inside snaffle ring under the chin to the outside;   d) on the chin strap between the inside and outside ring

As the work progresses the side reins are shortened to ask for more flexion and contact with the bit. The difference between the inside and outside rein can be as much as 5 to 8 cm, or about 3 to 5 holes, depending on the size of the horse. The outside rein should be adjusted so that it is taut and should complement the inside rein and stop the horse from falling out onto its outside shoulder.

The lunge rein is about 7 m long with a loop for the hand at the end. There are also lunge reins up to 10 m in length. They have the advantage that the horse can go in a larger circle. The lunge whip should be long enough for the trainer to reach the horse with the end of the cord. The stick and its thong together should be 5 to 6 m.

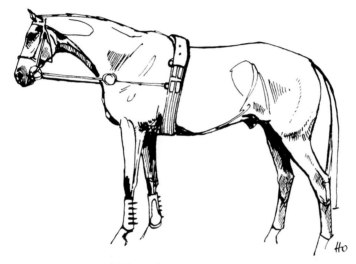

A horse correctly fitted out for lungeing

THE FIRST LUNGE LESSON The first lunge lesson should be carried out where the horse is least distracted, so if possible choose an indoor school. If this is not available, try to find a place where at least two to three sides of the circle have a natural barrier.

To begin with we do not use the lunge whip but we leave it in the tack room. On the morning of the first lunge lesson it is best to turn the horse out in the school so that it can get rid of some of its energy. Later in the afternoon, we put on the lunge tack and take the horse into the school. The groom comes as well and leads the horse with his left hand on the side of the bridle while the trainer walks on the inside of a small circle. The trainer holds the lunge line loosely with his right hand free to pat and reassure the horse when needed.

After walking round a few times the trainer slowly releases the lunge line and walks slowly to the centre of the circle. He stays on the spot and turns with the movement of the horse. Slowly he establishes a rein contact with the horse. The groom then starts to let go of the bridle every now and again until the horse remains on the circle by itself. The trainer will stop frequently and walk up to the horse on the circle and pat it.

The first lunge lesson is finished. The groom removes the side reins and leads the horse back into the stable. Some may ask: "Is this all you do the first time you lunge?". The answer is "Yes", as the more time you take at the beginning the easier it will be later. Young riders are apt to be sceptical about these old principles because they are impatient. It is quite understandable that they want to achieve quick results but a good instructor ensures that ambition does not take over but without stifling it.

PROGRESSIVE TRAINING   The next day we take the lunge whip with us and put it down in the middle of the circle or keep it tucked under one arm. The exercise starts as the day before. After a little while the trainer picks up the whip and tries to get the horse used to it by pointing it in the direction of the hind legs so that the horse is brought between the lunge rein and whip. The groom still keeps hold of the horse until it has settled down. When it starts to trot he stays with it, quietly talking to it but then slowly falls back.

The trainer points the whip in the direction of the horse's hind legs and is prepared to encourage the horse with a touch on the croup at the same time as calling "trot" if it should fall back to walk. Otherwise he just lets it trot around a few times until it has settled and the horse will go back to walk on its own, if not, continuing until it does.

If the horse trots on the circle on its own, the second lesson has been learned. The lesson should be finished off with a walk. We do not ask for canter yet.

If the young horse has learned to stay on the circle on its own the groom can come to the inside of the circle and stay near it by its girth. If the horse stops the groom steps up to it and leads it on again, while the trainer encourages it at the same time with a slight tap of the whip and saying "trot". If the horse has trotted well on the circle the day before, it is not necessary for the groom to help. We only need him again when we want to change the rein. This can create new problems – depending on the temperament of the horse. As most horses prefer to go on the left rein we always start that way.

It may be necessary when changing the rein for the first time to have the groom help again in the same way as on the first day. One should treat each young horse according to its intelligence and willingness.

As a rule 8 to 10 days is the time necessary to get the horse used to going on the lunge on both reins.

We continue the work on the lunge to maximise obedience and balance before starting riding. The trainer has to rely on his eye and feelings as he has not yet had bodily contact. The lunge whip serves to get the horse used to whip and leg. Rein aids are transmitted through the lunge rein, cavesson and side reins.

Lungeing a young horse in working trot. The lunge line maintains contact and the side reins allow the horse's neck to be stretched forwards and downwards

Most lungeing is done at working trot. Cantering should not be started for at least a week. The canter should be developed from the trot with a little help from the whip and giving the command "canter" – this may have to be repeated a few times – and is supported by the raising of the lunge line. Five to ten rounds are enough in this pace. Several short canters on the circle improve this pace better than a long period. The trot should follow the canter and then walk. At the end of the session I remove the side reins.

The object of lungeing has been achieved when the horse walks, trots and canters quietly accepting the contact with the side reins with his head and neck reaching forward and downwards.

It will be more easily understood now that all this takes time as we have gone through the lessons step by step.

4 Loose Schooling

When I was at the Westfalischen Reit und Fahr-schule I often used to let the young horses go free in the small school in preparation for their work over cavalletti. At first, without side reins, and then with them. The small school was the most suitable as it only measured 18 × 36 m and the trainer was able to stand in the middle of the school where his voice and lunge whip were still effective. This work was a lot of fun and we used to call it our circus school. All this was much easier than lungeing as the horses work on their own and are not restricted by the lunge rein. As preparation and completion of the education of the young unmounted horse I highly recommend this "circus school", as long as the school is not larger than 20 × 40 m.

We divided the work into two phases and added trotting over cavalletti later on. As preparation for a horse soon to be ridden the first two phases – letting loose and putting on side reins – are quite sufficient as it would be too soon to ask for more. Our target at this stage is to get on the back of the horse.

Letting loose

To begin this first phase put one cone in each corner about 2 m from the track and then lead the horse into the school with boots or bandages, snaffle bridle with reins rolled up and attached to the throat lash and saddle with stirrups removed or lunge roller and let it move freely about the school. Put the side reins in the middle of the school. Take the stirrup leathers off the saddle.

We first observe how the horse behaves when it is free after coming out of the stable and let him have his bit of fun. We stay in the middle of the school and bide our time. Usually any horse settles after 5 to 10 minutes and begins to listen to our voice and then we can start. If it takes longer for him to settle we just wait and talk to him quietly. When we have caught him, he gets a pat and a tit-bit. This will lead to greater attachment and make it easier to catch the horse next time. Horses will come to you when offered a tit-bit. They soon get used to it.

The position of the bollards when exercising horses free in the school

Putting on the side reins

Now we start with the more serious work of the second phase. We put on the side reins. These should enable the snaffle bit to lie quietly in the horse's mouth and get him to accept it with confidence. The side reins should help to make the horse stretch its neck forward and down thereby rounding its back. They must therefore not be too short, but on the other hand not so long that there is no contact.

Naturally the reins must be of equal length as in contrast to lungeing we want the horse to go straight forward.

If the horse's neck is set rather low and he is developing muscles under the neck it may be advisable to use a third rein. This is fitted by fastening it to the girth and then through the legs to the noseband or a strap between the snaffle rings. This rein stops the nasty habit of a horse bobbing its head up

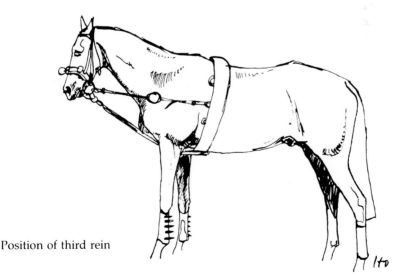

Position of third rein

39

and down and is also a correction for not wanting to stretch its neck forward and down.

Now let the horse trot and canter loose in the school with side reins. Quite soon we will see how it looks for support of the walls and will stay on the track with the help of the groom in the middle and the cones. It takes some horses only about 5 minutes to go willingly along the walls. Some take longer and it may need two people to help. The quieter the trainer and groom can be, the sooner the horse will settle.

This is an opportunity to study the horse's character and assess its intelligence, willingness and ability to learn quickly, or whether it will be resistant. At the same time, one should check one's own actions and realise that patience and time are the foundation of successful riding.

My experience has shown that after a while horses go along the sides of the school looking for support. As soon as this happens, further training can be introduced. The horse is working of its own accord. It goes along the track in the pace required and waits for the voice and whip to tell it whether to increase speed or stay as it is. To keep the horse happy in its work, I recommend that it should not work in trot longer than 5 minutes. If and when I let it canter is dependent on the progress of the training. I certainly

Work is starting in earnest. The young horse is tacked up with saddle, bridle and side reins which help to balance its trot

Two people help to keep the horse on the track when loose in the school

do not ask for canter on the first day unless the horse goes into canter by itself. I am satisfied when the horse trots in a regular rhythm along the walls of the school and is willing to lengthen the stride when asked. To do this I point the lunge whip at the croup and perhaps go along with the horse for a few steps.

The lesson will finish after about 20 minutes which includes both phases. Take off the side reins and then walk the horse until dried off and relaxed. Only then take it back to the stable.

5 Backing

It needs special skill to get up on the young horse for the first time. Even the quietest of horses can get frightened when it suddenly sees a big shadow behind it and shortly after that feels a strange weight on its back. One has to realise that the young horse has first to become accustomed to the weight of the rider on its back which will entail using nearly all its muscles. The neck, back and stomach muscles have to support its backbone. A completely green horse is often not physically strong enough which leads to stiffening of its neck and back, which in turn causes stumbling, pulling and other disturbances. This is the reason why we must not set our sights too high on this first day. We should be satisfied if the horse gets used to the rider getting up and off again. When talking of first mounting of the horse we mean just that, and nothing else. Anything else belongs to the basic training.

Mounting

There are trainers who keep their horses in the stable when they are first being mounted. I consider this an excessive safety measure and I only resort to it in exceptional cases. In these cases I put on the snaffle and lead the horse into its stable and put its back to the feed bin. The horse's usual groom stands to the left of it and takes hold of the reins, which are over its head, with his left hand. The rider approaches the horse and strokes it as though he was going to groom it. As soon as the horse accepts this the groom, with his right hand just below the rider's knee, lifts the rider carefully. The rider first lies across the horse's back. If the horse remains quiet, he lifts his right leg over the horse's rump and sits down but leans forward in order not to frighten the horse. After a few moments he gets off again gently. This exercise can be repeated a few times and a small reward (sugar or carrots for example) given after getting off. After this the saddle is put on and the horse is lead into the school.

Normally the getting on and off can be started in the school with a saddle on, as long as the horse has been prepared for this with its lunge work.

On the day when it is proposed to mount the horse for the first time, it should be lunged on both reins and then a little more on the left rein so that it is a bit tired when the rider gets up. It is a good idea to put on a neck-strap which the rider can use to catch hold if the horse should buck.

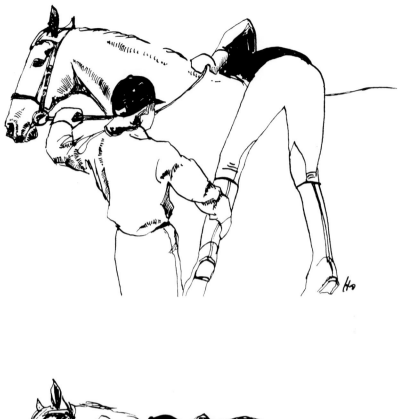

Becoming used to the rider getting up and down: (*top*) the rider lies over the horse's back: (*bottom*) the rider sits astride but stays forward for the time being 43

For the actual backing, the horse retains its lungeing equipment

It is my experience that it is best to move the horse forwards as soon as the rider is in the saddle. The groom should lead the horse onto the lungeing circle to which it is used. If this is done it is very unlikely that there will be unpleasant surprises. The rider follows the horse's movements but is completely passive and gives no aids. The horse will usually start trotting and the rider rises to the trot and leans slightly forwards. The horse will probably tire after a few rounds and stop trotting. The groom who was lungeing steps up to the horse making it halt. The rider should feel when the horse has had enough so after this first halt he can stop, or carry on for a little longer – according to how the horse feels. It depends entirely on how the horse reacts. If the horse has settled down the rider should get on and off a further one or two times. Nothing else should be attempted on the first day.

When being ridden for the first time, it is a good idea to use a quiet lead horse which has been in the school when the young horse was being lunged. If it is brought in later it will only unsettle the youngster and it is best for the older horse to walk about one horselength in front of the young horse as soon as its rider is mounted. This is done best on the left rein, along the boards to stop the young horse from falling out, and not on the circle. The young horse should follow in the tracks of the lead horse with the person lungeing staying near to it to be at hand if necessary. After walking for a while, they can start trotting. The rest of the exercise is the same as without the lead horse. If possible the lesson should end with the rider getting on and off once or twice more.

The rider's weight

It is important for the rider to remember that the horse has first to become used to carrying the rider's weight. It is advisable, therefore, to carry on as above for at least one to two weeks before starting anything new. In the first week the horse should be lunged for a short while before being ridden. We do not ride our young horses every day. Every other day we lunge them, let them go free in the school and use the days when they are not ridden to get them used to cavalletti without the rider. I will not go into detail about the latter as it is discussed later.

We use the days when they are not ridden to strengthen the muscles with exercises to make it easier for them to carry the rider. Even so they will be a bit stiff to begin with but that will go as the muscles strengthen.

The muscles of the back will not be strengthened by riding a horse often and long. Muscles will only develop when a horse has careful and well thought out work. If asked to do more than it is physically able to do it will only stiffen up, stop growing and permanent damage could be done. That is why we are very careful not to ride young horses too often or for too long, and to intersperse it with gymnastic exercises, such as getting on and off, lungeing, running free in the school, leading them over small obstacles etc.

Getting the horse used to a rider on its back. One assistant holds the horse's head and another quietly and quickly lifts the rider into the saddle

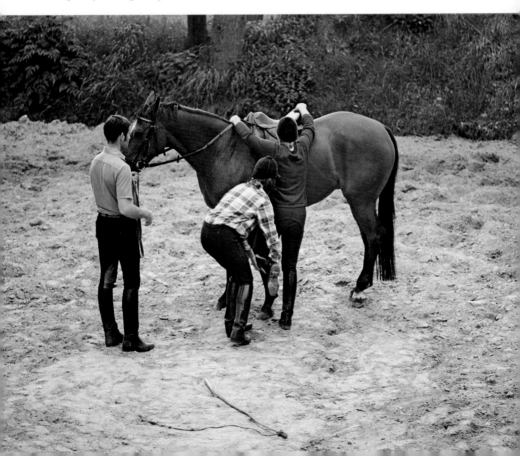

There is no definite place for the saddle on the back of a young horse, so we have to be very careful to find and keep the correct position, adjusting it if necessary. It will slowly develop – sometimes it can take months, depending on the shape of the wither and shoulder. A fore girth can be used to keep the saddle in position but I do not advise its use during the first few weeks, as it would mean an extra girth, which might upset the young horse. The breastplate often pinches, as it has to be put on very tight to prevent slipping. We can dispense with the idea of a breastplate when we realise that we are only at the beginning of the horse's education, only teaching it to carry the rider's weight. The horse only needs the breastplate later on when we are teaching it the aids by changing our weight in the saddle. The saddle may then slip into the wrong position.

We must be satisfied with trot and walk on both reins to begin with. It is quite useful to have a lead horse for the first few minutes or at least after first getting on. We stay on straight lines or follow the lead horse on a large circle. The young horse is ridden for 10 to 15 minutes only, during the first week, especially if it is lunged beforehand. In the second week the trot work can be increased to 20 to 30 minutes with two or three short walk phases when changing rein. We have achieved our first goal when the horse carries us willingly in walk and trot.

Riding the young horse on the lunge. The rider adjusts his movements to the horse and interferes as little as possible. The person lungeing guides the horse and is assisted by a helper

The light seat (young horse in trot)

In the first few weeks the trot should always be ridden rising, with the rider sitting slightly forward and as lightly as possible. The hands are low on either side of the horse's neck and take up a light contact with the horse's mouth. If the horse feels unsettled or changes its rhythm, close the knees tightly on the saddle, take hold of the neck strap with one hand and do not hold onto the reins. To do this would only make the horse run on more and set its jaw.

Should the rider be bucked off, he must get on again straight away or find a more experienced rider to take over. If he lets the young horse get away with bucking as a means of ridding it of the unpleasant weight on its back, this may encourage it to try again when it has the chance.

The rider's ambition, when first riding a young horse should be to merge his movements with those of the horse. He does not start giving aids, as the horse will not understand them. He uses voice and whip to regulate the speed and the whip is used on the shoulder. The spurs are left behind as they would be an interference. The voice should not be used too much. To speak to the horse all the time is unnecessary and can even be detrimental. The horse can remember short commands and words but continuous talking can only be unsettling and will not be understood.

6 The Principles of Basic Training

There are certain principles for the basic training of the young horse, after backing, which must be adhered to in order to avoid mental and physical damage to the horse. In Germany there is a Scale of Basic Training Principles which is fundamental to the examination for Bereiters (professional riders) and which everybody should know who wants to train a horse. The six principles in the Training Scale are "losgelassenheit", rhythm, contact, "schwung", straightness and collection. Following this training scale is the right way to develop the horse's natural abilities.

The systematic build up of the basic training is based on the knowledge of classical riding and was laid down in the rules of the German cavalry. It is the most important chapter on the theme of training as everything is built upon this.

The most important factor is to gain influence over the horse's movements and not to be satisfied with one's ability to adapt to the movement of the horse. I do not follow the "natural training method" which restricts itself to not disturbing the horse and allowing it to work on its own. This is fine if all goes well, but not if there are difficulties and resistances. I need true obedience, a state which is covered by the term "durchlassig" and although it is not included in the Scale of Basic Training Principles, it is an important part of my system. I ask for it after "losgelassenheit" and rhythm.

The training scale

In the following pages I would like to introduce the principles referred to in the Training Scale and put them into context within the system of basic training before dealing with them in more detail in later chapters.

"LOSGELASSENHEIT" We start by developing *losgelassenheit* which means a horse which freely gives all its muscles to use its whole body without any resistance; the horse is supple and unconstrained.

Before a horse is "losgelassenheit" we cannot start to build up the muscles or the training of the horse because our aim is to develop the natural movement. To achieve "losgelassenheit" we must make the movements of the young horse when it comes out of the stable the same as in nature when it was in the field. We must realise that the newly stabled horse gets stiff for it is not used to standing in a restricted space for nearly 23 hours of the day. In nature the horse is a moving animal so when we put a horse in a stable it is in an unnatural state and becomes stiff. We must bring this stiffness out before we can build up the training – this is the idea of "losgelassenheit".

After achieving "losgelassenheit" then the real work starts. Many riders spend too long with their horses long and low trying to make them perfectly "losgelassenheit". They have the wrong idea of "losgelassenheit" for the horse ends up going on its forehand and loses the natural brilliance of its gaits. Thus there is a danger in concentrating too much on "losgelassenheit".

RHYTHM   The logical result of becoming "losgelassenheit" is that the horse will move in a rhythm which is constant (same tempo), and correct (regular) for each pace (in German this is known as "takt"). After the freshness and tension has been taken out of the horse then it becomes a little lazy and the rider can apply the aids. The horse is then going naturally (supple in the back and not stiff). When it does this the rider can start to influence it in order to establish the natural rhythm of its movement.

Nature has given the horse three paces – the walk, trot and canter. These paces have their special sequences. The walk is four-time, the trot two-time and the canter three-time. To maintain the natural sequence, in other words the correct rhythm of the pace (regularity) and with a constant repetition (even tempo), is what is called in German "takt". To regulate it is the most important duty of the rider on the young horse. This is achieved through the rider's smooth adaptation to the movement to help the horse find its balance. To establish the correct, constant rhythm ("takt") the rider must get his horse balanced.

In the field the horse has a natural balance but when the rider adds his weight the greater burden falls on the front legs which puts excessive strain on them. The old maxim of a balanced load (i.e. equal distribution on the four legs) being easier to carry than an unbalanced one makes it imperative to bring the horse into a balance where the weight is more evenly distributed.

Working the horse long and low brings out the stiffness but when it becomes a little lazy then we should get it into a balance which is not on its fore hand. We need to make the back supple, and riding long and low is an easy way to do this, but we must remember that when long and low the horse is out of balance, if we take balance to mean that the weight is equally distributed on all four legs. The horse will have more weight on its fore hand and in training we work to gradually change the balance, to make its hind quarters stronger so that it can carry more weight with them and give the shoulders the freedom to extend and to show brilliance in the gaits.

The way the rider gets his horse balanced is very important. In the beginning he should concentrate on "losgelassenheit" and establish rhythm, then use careful aids to help the hind quarters come under the   49 horse to achieve better balance. If the rider asks too much, too early, the paces will simply speed up, and if he sits too heavy the horse will drop its back down. In the early stages the natural feel of the rider is important so he can remain "with" the horse.

To establish the rhythm the horse has to learn to carry and balance the rider's weight so that it can move freely and without strain. When this is achieved one says the horse moves in a natural balance, and with a constant, correct rhythm ("takt").

The more influence the rider wants to gain over the horse's movements the more he has to concern himself with the training of the horse to accept the forward, lateral and restraining aids. Obedience to these aids is called "Durchlassigkeit". A horse is "durchlassig" when it is "losgelassen" and obedient to the rider's forward driving, lateral and restraining aids. The more trained the horse the lighter the aids should be. When teaching, the aids may have to be obvious but riders should recognise that this is only a stage and gradually apply them lighter and lighter.

With each new thing taught the aids may have to be strong so the horse makes the effort. This is not cruel. We do not work with whips and spurs. If I feel the horse does not understand then I go back a stage but many riders lose their reason when this happens, get angry and go on demanding. Eventually they may get obedience out of a tired horse but they will not get it the next day. We want to influence the horse but this must not be at the price of destroying it. When the horse is tired we must stop training because a tired horse cannot put expression and brilliance into its work. We must not mechanise the horse.

CONTACT   A major principle of basic training is to build up the "schwung" – to add cadence and impulsion to the gaits. A horse which is fresh in the field can have "schwung" but only for a few steps, and what we want to do is to cultivate this natural ability by correctly developing the muscles which run from the hind quarters over the back and neck. The "schwung" can only be built up when the horse moves with rhythm and the rider has a *contact* with the horse's mouth. If we just push the horse it runs and loses its rhythm. It may be trotting forward, even have the desire to go forward, but there is no "schwung". A condition for developing "schwung" is contact between the rider's hands and the horse's mouth. First we must train the horse so we can establish contact with the mouth and then we can influence it. We need the contact to produce the "schwung", to develop all the ability which is in the horse.

Contact is not only to the mouth, because this is only one of the three aids, apart from the hands there are also leg and weight aids. To develop the contact we need to teach the horse all the aids through forward riding, the half-halts, leg yielding and transitions. These are the steps on the way to establishing a contact.

The horse needs to learn the aids of the legs, weight and hands, and all
three must work together in co-ordination and must explain to the horse that

the aids are to go forwards, to go laterally and to restrain. The horse must learn first these fundamental aids and before this is achieved we cannot ask for "schwung" (and, later, collection) because we cannot really influence the horse.

Contact does not mean that by pulling the reins we will have it. The horse should step into the contact and establish an outline corresponding to the respective pace; an outline within which it can best develop its power. This is the aim of stepping into the contact. The rider's legs, weight and hands bring the horse into a form within which it can carry itself so that it can move most comfortably. Then it will be able to move, when it is muscled up, to the best of its ability.

The ultimate objective of contact should be that it is even on both sides of the mouth, but this takes time. Even at advanced levels of dressage the horse usually has one good and one bad side. When the feel in both hands is equal the horse is well trained. The trainer should be happy in the beginning even if the contact is better on one side of the mouth than the other. If he concentrates too much in trying to even up the contact it makes the horse too loose in front of the wither. He must never forget that the work starts from behind. Contact is established as a result of the horse working from behind and the trainer should ride his horse from behind, build up the muscles in the hind quarters and over the back and then, when he applies driving aids, will be able to feel it in the hand.

Usually one will have more contact in one hand than the other and if the hands are held steady then the contact will eventually improve, but if the hands are wriggled then there is the danger of riding from the front to the back, the rhythm will be lost and the movement will not come from the quarters over the back to the hand.

"SCHWUNG"   With the help of contact we can improve the "schwung". A horse looks its best under a rider only when it is evident that the hind quarters push off with energy and spring, and that the power generated in trot or canter is conducted forward through the swinging rounded back of the horse – the horse is working "through". That is what we call "schwung".

The aim in dressage is more "schwung" so that we have more expression to the movement. We like to cultivate the natural gaits, to give them more expression, balance, brilliance and cadence so that the horse can stay longer in the air, but without stiffness or flicking of the legs. Each leg must bend at the joints and step onto the ground where it points. We might see this in nature but only for moments, we want to cultivate this natural ability by building up the muscles so that the horse can produce it with ease.

"Schwung" enables the horse to move in the most expressive way that nature gave it. Some horses by nature have little expression, i.e. have flat gaits. One must remember that one can only ride out of a horse what nature gave it, but what nature gave it we want to bring out. This means the horse must be able to use all four legs with maximum expression and to do this   51 entails engaging the hind legs through muscling up the hind quarters so it is easy to engage them. Many people forget that the shoulders are also important and should not be stiff. They need to develop free movement. The expression comes from behind but if it cannot go through the back and through the shoulders because the shoulders are stiff then again there is no "schwung".

STRAIGHTNESS   Ride your horse forward and put it *straight*. This is our next training aim. Experts have discovered that nearly all young horses have difficulties in going straight. One talks of the natural crookedness of the horse. As most people are right handed so are most horses bent to the left. According to Müseler the reason for this is the position of the foal in the womb. It is therefore very important in the basic training to even out this natural crookedness by balanced training on both sides so that the fore legs are adjusted onto the track of the hind legs. This is what is called straightening the horse.

In the early stages of basic training "schwung" is more important than getting the horse straight. When making the horse straight one must realise that in nature the horse is not straight. It is born crooked so we have to correct a little bit of its natural movement. We cannot say that it is natural to be straight but the horse must eventually go straight because we want it to be so and if the horse is straight it moves better. We can start early to make little corrections, but to do the work to make it permanently straight then the horse must have reached a relatively advanced stage in the training. The young horse can only be made straight at the expense of losing expression in its movements. First we should establish contact and continue to develop a better contact as we make little corrections to its straightness. To make the horse absolutely straight we need to work with diagonal aids and cannot do so unless it understands the aids. We can only make a horse straight when we have established the four earlier principles.

We must be careful when making the horse straight not to bend it in front of the withers. We must not loosen the muscles in front of the withers for we need to build up either side of the neck so it is steady in front of the withers. We need a steady feel in our reins so if we take the right rein the horse flexes and goes right and does not simply bend in front of the withers and lets the shoulder fall out. We must be able to ride a horse rather like a bicycle.

COLLECTION   The basic training finishes when *collection* starts. It is the last of the principles because first we must make the horse free and more muscular. To collect it we need to restrain and change the distribution of the weight. Collection entails putting more weight onto the hind legs through the lowering of the quarters and hocks which enables the horse to use its full potential strength. The more weight there is on the hind legs the freer are the shoulders and therefore the easier it is for the horse to shift its point of balance backwards. This is important not only for dressage but equally for jumping and cross country, for example when taking off for a jump.

In the basic training we do not ask too high a standard of any of the principles. The principles must be fulfilled but not maximised, and they are developed further when specialisation takes place. Later we can be more critical and ask for more from the horse.

It is important for the horse to establish a basic understanding of the principles but not to be forced in its training. Therefore the trainer should not become too bogged down in detail nor be insistent that the horse *must* do it. The principles need to be seen within the whole spectrum of basic training; and the horse developed so it will be able to specialise in the field in which it is most talented.

7 The Fundamentals of a Lesson

The progressive build up of basic training is how we develop the horse's natural abilities. It would be foolish, however, to think that a young horse could be trained by one day practising the "losgelassenheit", the next day the rhythm and the third the contact etc. Nor can all the principles be practised in the hour or so of the lesson. We have stated principles, now we have to combine them in a riding lesson for that day. That can mean that we will concentrate on the rhythm, or making the horse straight but we cannot ride everything. We have to make a choice as to what we do that day. This can change every day, or even during the working section as if something is not successful then we have to change to something else. The riders must have flexibility, i.e. have a planned line to follow but can change if this does not work, although this does not apply so much with trained horses as with young horses.

When planning the lesson the trainer should bear in mind that the principles of the Training Scale can be pursued not just when working on the flat but also when jumping or going across country. I develop the principles within the context of the entire system of basic training. Only then will the training be comprehensive and create the foundation for the full development of the abilities of the horse.

When starting with new exercises we must take the horse's character and ability into consideration. We must be careful that it enjoys its work and must not let the work become repetitive as repetition makes for boredom and dullness. The lessons must be made interesting and varied. If possible, and weather allowing, it is a good idea to change the place where the horse is working. For example, I start off in the indoor school with cavalletti and then go out into the country, or I go out first and on my return go into the school to work through a few dressage exercises. Sometimes I gallop the horse on a racetrack and after that go into the dressage arena. Both rider and horse must enjoy the work. This is the essence of success.

There are three sections to every lesson – the loosening up, the work, and then the drying off and relaxing, and it is only in the work section that the rider has to decide how to combine the principles and which ones to concentrate on that particular day. If this pattern of three sections to the lesson is adhered to it will save many disappointments.

An important exercise for loosening the horse is to walk on a long rein. The 4-year-old Trakehner gelding "Optimist" by "Major" is ridden by Ruth Klimke. The horse's tail is still clamped down

Each lesson begins with "loosening up". Only a horse which has "losgelassenheit" is in a position to move freely and naturally immediately. It takes longer for a young horse to achieve this state, as the muscles must get stronger before the horse is able to carry the rider without discomfort. That is why, during the first few weeks of training we spend more time doing the loosening up exercises than anything else.

To loosen up the horse we walk on a loose rein. The rider sits still and waits until the horse walks on quietly without hurrying. One or two cavalletti are useful to make the horse stretch its neck and head forward and down. At the beginning the tail is often clamped down tightly but slowly it should be carried more naturally and this is an indication that the muscles are relaxing.

If the horse is fresh when it comes out of the stable and has not been lunged it often makes it very difficult to establish true "losgelassenheit" in the walk. It depends on the horse's temperament but one can by trotting satisfy the horse's need to go forward and usually calm it down a little. It is best to start with rising trot and on the left rein. If the horse has learned the rein aids, I prefer to go on a circle to quieten it down. The rider follows the movements of the horse, quietens it, if necessary uses his voice and concentrates only on establishing the rhythm.

To loosen up a young horse takes about 15 to 20 minutes. As the education continues this time gets shorter and shorter so that we can progress to the work section more quickly, but we should never neglect this first section completely. There are some riders who believe that once a horse is ridden it does not need to be loosened up, that this process makes it go on its fore hand and it is useless to loosen the horse and get rid of the tension which is of use later in the piaffe and passage. Such misguided ideas can only occur when the complete system of riding education has not been studied in its entirety. The horses prove this, become irregular in the walk, tight in the back, and take tense steps – these are the unmistakeable signs that a horse has not been loosened up for a long time.

For the first six weeks the loosening up section takes most of the lesson, but we progress to include the second section – "the work": As soon as the horse is loosened up we can start to work it, to develop the obedience of the horse to the aids of our hands, legs and seat. This is done in the school, out in the country or jumping. We prepare a carefully planned programme for each day, according to the progress the horse is making, starting with simple exercises and slowly building up to the more difficult.

We must be prepared to come to a dead end sometimes. No trainer is perfect and even the most experienced rider makes mistakes. The most important thing is to realise this and to try and correct errors as quickly as possible. Should the horse, for example, switch off when it is not able to

An aid to help the horse to loosen up is to walk over cavalletti on a loose rein. Heinz Brüggemann on "Maraschino", a 4-year-old Hanoverian by "Maikater"

Rising trot on the circle with a long, low and forward stretched neck. This creates "losgelassenheit" and forward movement at the beginning of the lesson. Reiner Klimke on the 5-year-old gelding "Maiko" by "Maigraf"

understand and carry out an exercise, it would be of no value to use force. As soon as I realise this has happened I stop the exercise immediately and go on to another – preferably easier – one to regain the horse's attention.

Horses are not able to pay attention to the riders aids for an indefinite period. For a young horse it is often unpleasant or even painful to work on the bit for any length of time. It should have short breaks and be allowed now and then to stretch its neck on a long rein. I recommend therefore, especially when riding a young horse, to have a break every 10 to 15 minutes and by doing this I hope to prevent any conflict with the horse.

My ideal is to finish the lesson on a good note, irrespective of whether it was an easy or difficult exercise; the horse will still thank me. I will have created a good starting point for the next day, as horses have excellent memories. This is the way to develop the lessons. If I finish with a well executed exercise I can take it up at the same point the next day. The experienced trainer uses this factor to his advantage.

The third section of the lesson is the "drying off". This is done at the walk on a long rein and, sadly, out of indifference, is often neglected. To let the horse dry off only requires patience from the rider, but for the horse it is very important. A horse that is allowed to dry off will be content to return to the stable. It will regain its inner peace even if there has been a bit of a battle when it was ridden. Also walking out on a long rein will help to establish a 57 rhythmic, forward walk. I have proved this point with the dressage and event horses that I trained.

It takes about 5 to 10 minutes to dry off a young horse, although it depends on how hard the horse has worked and how much it has taken out of itself. Let us never forget: the horse which has had time to relax and dry off will start off the next day's work in a happy and responsive frame of mind.

8 Control of the Work

It is important to adjust the work to suit the horse. When riding it is not always easy to realise that one is asking too much. Nervous and lively horses, especially, give the impression that it is impossible to tire them out but this is often a mistaken impression and it is important to visit the stable a few hours after riding to check the horse. If it is standing listlessly this usually proves that it has been asked to do too much and the demands made of it must then be reduced immediately. Listlessness, however, may not be due to exhaustion but to a change of feeding or to teeth that are too sharp so that the horse cannot chew properly. If we think this is the case the vet should be called to rasp the teeth and get rid of the sharpness.

Nothing is as important as the horse's legs. Tendons and joints must be constantly watched. If there is any heat in the legs or swelling in the joints it is a clear indication that the horse has been doing too much. An experienced groom should notice if something is wrong. When looking after the horse he should feel each leg for warmth and if the horse seems generally a little under the weather he should take its temperature. Before riding the horse the trainer should ask if all is well with it and to satisfy himself he can feel its legs.

To prevent swelling it is a good idea to wash the horse's legs and feet after work – weather permitting – and then to massage them a little with a flat hand working down the tendons to the fetlock. No more should be done, such as applying a blister or medication, until the vet has been consulted. This should not be necessary with a young horse unless it has done exceptionally hard work.

As well as keeping an eye on the legs, one must make certain that the feet are regularly examined. To prevent them from drying up, hoof oil should be applied after the feet have been washed. If the going is good it is not necessary to have young horses shod until they go to their first show unless the shapes of the feet have to be corrected. The blacksmith who regularly trims the feet should be consulted about this. If the ground is varied it should suffice to have the front feet only shod. This is what I usually do and find that it works very well.

9 Working Towards the Development of "Schwung"

Having loosened the horse and obtained "losgelassenheit", we now want to make the young horse familiar with the rider's aids so we can influence it and develop "schwung". Apart from the voice and whip there are the aids of weight, leg and hand. To teach these to the horse there are certain exercises through which the horse can learn obedience to individual aids and the effect of their co-ordination. These exercises are those found in the dressage tests Kl. A. in Germany (novice in England). The further training programme for dressage is tested in L, M and S tests in Germany (elementary, medium and advanced in England). Each grade of test represents a certain stage in the horse's education and the training for each grade should take about a year.

Some people think that they can train a horse by going over and over a test until the horse can do it, but then they have not understood the idea behind the basic training. The tests are only a means to an end and not an end in themselves. We want to promote the horse's natural abilities with gymnastic exercises, and by doing this we want to make the horse healthier and more beautiful. We do not want to be just good test riders.

I cannot emphasise enough that horses which go through tests over and over again get dull and lose their "oomph". Sadly we often see horses at shows that are obedient but have lost their sparkle and "schwung". The danger of this is not to be ignored in Germany. The difficulty is that because of the ever increasing number of starters in competitions the tests have had to be shortened which lays greater emphasis on each movement.

The shorter tests increase the danger of forgetting the major principles which is the development of the gaits, the movement of the horse. The horse is not given the chance to settle and go around the arena in a working pace. The short tests start immediately with figures and it becomes more and more like a circus. When the German Federation revised the tests attention was paid to the great importance of the correctness of the paces, especially in more novice tests. The judges and test makers have a great responsibility towards the standard of training. They give the lines which will help riders to pursue principles and these must be the right principles. They should not be looking for mistakes at this stage of training, but whether the horse is being made into an athlete. Inattentiveness is not serious because we do not want to mechanise the horse. Many judges look for mistakes rather than purity of the paces and the correct way of going. The horse which is technically right should never be beaten by a horse which is not technically right but made no mistakes. In training we must be encouraged to first establish the principles and only then to tackle the details.

Obedience to the forward aids

We will turn our attention again to the training of the young horse. Once we have settled the young horse we start working on its acceptance of the forward driving aids. We can use a stronger lower leg close to the girth, perhaps aided by a slight touch of the whip and use of the voice. If the horse does not react we must strengthen the aids.

By repeating this exercise over and over again using leg, whip and voice we try to reach the stage when only the leg is needed and we can do without the whip and voice, only using the latter if the horse does not react to the leg.

The forward aids are indispensable when developing a strong hind leg which will come well under the horse. These aids on their own, however, are not enough. Pushing forward does not develop an active hind leg on its own: for this we need to establish a soft contact between the rider's hands and the horse's mouth. The horse must step into the bit and position its head and neck where it can best develop its movements according to its strength.

Putting the horse on the bit

How does one put a horse on the bit? It is practically impossible to explain this in a few sentences. It is not enough just to take hold of the reins and make contact with the horse's mouth. Through ignorance the horse would react in exactly the opposite way to what we are hoping. It would resist and set its jaw or bolt. The only way to achieve success is by combining the weight and leg aids with those of the hands.

The secret of the influence man has over the horse is based on the combination of weight, legs and hands.

I combine my rein aids with a light pressure of the thigh and a stronger seat. Up to now, in the first phase of riding a young horse, I used a very light hand to enable the horse to stretch its neck forward, but now comes the time when a stronger contact is required to make the horse step into the bit. The forward driving aids create an active trot. The rider's hands go with the movement and must not be so heavy that they restrict the movement from the hind legs going "through" the back and to the mouth. This requires sensitive hands and a great deal of feel. The rider has to be very careful at the beginning not to use force to pull the horse on the bit, as this would only 61

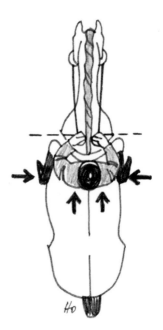

Aids to put the horse on the bit

create resistance and problems. With a soft and sensitive hand we must try to find the correct contact with the horse's mouth and make it as pleasant as possible for the horse. To do this a flexible wrist is essential. With good hands the contact will be improved and through good training eventually reach such a stage that the horse will step "through" with no resistance to block it in the hind quarters, back, neck or jaw.

It is not possible to achieve this in one day. It depends on the development of the activity of the hind leg, on the ability of the horse to work "through", which helps the horse to carry its head and neck higher so that the rider has more in front of him. We have to work on every aspect of the horse's education in order to improve the horse's desire to step into the contact.

The movement of the horse comes from behind to the front "through" a soft swinging back and our full attention must be directed towards this. When riding the young horse it should always work from behind forwards and not the other way around from in front to behind. Necks that have been pulled in stop the muscles on the back developing and interfere with the natural paces. The result is the opposite to what we are trying to do in our basic training. I mention this as it is at this point that the path divides, leading either to success or failure in the horse's education. If we try to force the horse's head and neck into a certain position too early we are heading in the wrong direction, and it will create difficulties in the future. I am thinking, for example, of horses which are overbent in the neck, unsteady in the mouth, tense in the back and thereby their temperaments are damaged. All of this leads to a shortness of the stride, a loss of rhythm and a tightness in the movements which will always be a handicap in further training.

To advance the work we need to make the horse familiar with and confident to the classical aids. We concentrate at this stage in teaching the horse to be obedient to forward, lateral and restraining aids. It is only when the horse accepts these aids that the rider can influence its movements on the straight and through corners.

The manner of applying the aids should have been part of the rider's education. The rider should have learnt them on an older trained horse, otherwise it is hardly possible to carry out the required work and there is great danger of mistakes being made. The young rider should work on a schooled horse and the experienced rider on a young horse. That is an old maxim of education.

Should someone buy a young horse and have little experience it is best if he can ride many other horses – if possible ones which are well-schooled. Money and time spent this way are a good investment. A rider who is lucky enough to ride various horses daily can draw comparisons and improve his reactions, which is an important part of training. Someone who does not have this opportunity must prepare himself with greater care by studying the theory in order to avoid as many riding mistakes as possible in the education of the horse, and to have the correct approach to the work.

Reiner Klimke riding the 4-year-old gelding "Volt" by "Vollkorn". He is teaching the horse to accept the bit and to do this at this stage in the training he keeps his hands steady so he is offering the bit to the horse to accept

Taking hold of the bit can create wrong flexion in the neck in spite of low hands and long reins

Trainers must be conversant with the following different exercises which help us to teach the horse obedience to our forward and restraining aids.

Obedience to the lateral aids

We have already discussed the forward driving aids used, for example, to ride forwards and to trot on. With these basic aids we have taught the horse to go forwards, trot on and to take the contact with the hand. We will now look at the lateral aids (sideways and forward movements).

TURN ON THE FORE HAND   An important lesson in the obedience to lateral movements is the turn on the fore hand. This is a loosening up movement and it is a useful exercise in between the work which makes a horse hot when the horse can get used to the effect of the lateral aids of the leg, a weight change and rein aids.

   To do this the rider halts the horse about 3 m from the wall on the left rein. He then puts more weight on his right seatbone and shortens the right rein. The first reaction he is aiming at is that the horse will give in the mouth when

Aids for the turn on the fore hand. This movement is started with the horse off the track, so he is a little way from the side of the school

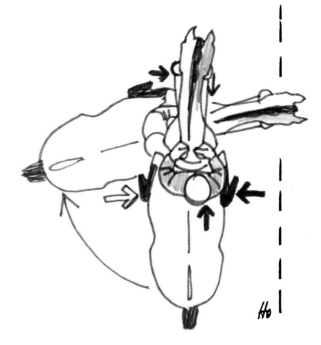

A turn on the fore hand in the middle of the school. Marijke Dommerholt on the Dutch chestnut gelding "Robijn"

it feels the shortening of the right rein. If it does this a little, praise with the voice but if not, shortening of the rein must be repeated. Next the rider uses some pressure with his right leg just behind the girth and pushes the hind legs step by step around the fore hand until the turn is complete. If the horse does not obey the leg I use the whip lightly just behind my leg. As a further help I turn the horse's head slightly to the right by giving and taking the reins on the right. The left leg stays on the horse behind the girth to control the hind quarters. To begin with I stop the horse after the first crossing of the hind legs and praise it. I then carry on this way until the turn has been completed. Should there be difficulties after the first crossing steps I always go back to the beginning asking for the appropriate bend.

Now that the young horse has been introduced to the lateral aids I pay special attention in future exercises to the shifting of my weight and the use of the outside rein. The heavier seat to one side stops the horse from stepping back. The outside rein stops the outside shoulder falling out and the horse from moving forward.

The turn on the fore hand can also be used as a correction, for example, a horse which will not go towards a jump or has become insensitive to the leg. The latter is often the result of continuous use of the lower leg, a nagging leg.

LEG YIELDING Leg yielding also belongs to the loosening up exercises which teach the horse to obey the rider's aids for the lateral movements. The value of this movement in the further education of the horse is debatable as like the turn on the fore hand it does not improve the paces and does not improve the cadence. Leg yielding is therefore only a preparatory exercise for future work.

Leg yielding is done at the walk and a shortened working trot but only for short distances. The rider gives the following aids: Leg yielding to the right – the left rein asks for a slight bend to the left, the side of the left lower leg "yields" the horse to the right, and if possible is applied at the moment the left hind leg lifts off. The rider puts more weight on his left seatbone. The right rein leads the fore hand and stops the right shoulder from falling out. The right lower leg stays firmly on the horse, behind the girth, and used more strongly if the horse wants to run away from the inside leg and starts to take hurried steps. If the horse is trying to evade the inside leg, the rider leads the fore hand a short step forward as if going to do a volte (small circle), but the hind legs stay on the same track. He then uses the aids as described at the beginning but the right rein is now the inside one and the right leg the one moving the horse sideways. The leg yield is finished by aligning the fore hand with the hind quarters by using the outside rein to straighten the horse.

The acceptance of the leg to move the horse laterally is of the greatest importance as it leads the way to the shoulder-in and the latter is an exercise which does help to develop the horse's cadence. The difference between the leg yield and the shoulder-in is that in the former the horse is at 45 degrees angle to the track and the shoulder-in not more than 30 degrees.

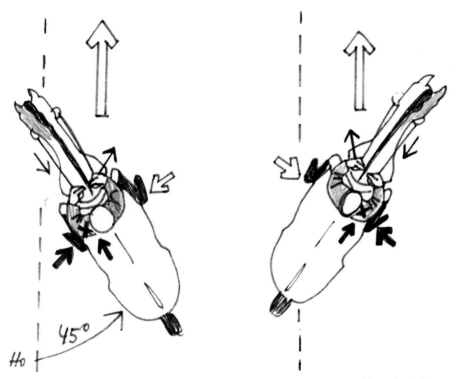

The aids for leg yielding: (*left*) leg yield to the right; (*right*) leg yield to the left

The right leg yielding. The horse moves away from the inside leg to make four tracks. With her legs the rider gives the horse a slight bend to the right, puts more weight on the right seatbone and keeps the left lower leg firmly behind the girth.

LINE-TO-LINE LEG YIELDING To establish the horse's obedience to the lateral aids, vary the length and width in line to line leg yielding. In this exercise the horse moves in leg yield in two tracks and the distance between the two tracks is one step (i.e. fore hand one step ahead of hind quarters), until it gets to one step before the change of direction. The easier it is for the horse to move laterally the easier it will be to change direction.

The exercise becomes gradually less of a loosening one to more of preparation for the half-passes. This preparation is of value and is why one should not belittle the leg yield.

In the beginning, to help the horse move laterally, we need a distinct bend, but the better the horse moves across the less the rider has to bend it, the straighter the horse can be kept and the closer the leg yield comes to a half-pass. This is of value.

How far the horse is asked to leg yield depends on the level of the horse's education. To begin with we ask for only a few steps. To execute this exercise the rider gives the following aids: after riding through the corner on the left rein, the rider gives the horse a slight position to the right. He then puts more weight on his right seatbone and puts his lower leg back a little. When starting the leg yielding after the corner the right leg pushes the horse so it yields forward and sideways to the middle of the school. The left leg stays in a positive contact and if necessary helps to keep the horse going forward. Having reached the centre line the horse is straightened up and ridden in a straight line for one horse length. The aids are then changed to those for the opposite direction. On reaching the long side the horse is straightened and the lesson is finished.

Leg yielding across the school. Good crossing of legs and correct bend to the left

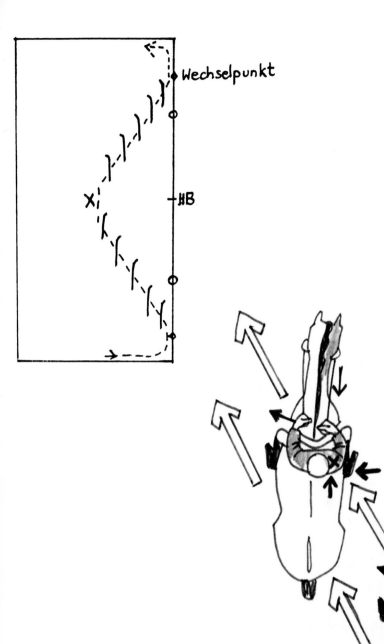

Wechselpunkt

HB

The aids in line-to-line leg yielding

Riding curved lines

As we have now taught our horse to listen to our lateral aids, in the turn on the fore hand and leg yield we can concentrate on riding circles and turns. This includes riding a corner correctly, voltes of a 10 m diameter, serpentines and changing the rein through the circle.

TURNS AND RIDING THROUGH CORNERS   Until the young horse has learned to bend properly, we cannot influence it in the turns. Aware of this we ride it in circles which are big so as not to disturb it and to enable it to keep the rhythm and activity of its hind legs. When it has learned to accept the lateral aids we can start giving it the bend that is necessary to engage its outside hind leg and not fall out.

How is this done? In each turn, the horse's outside legs have to cover more ground than the inside pair. This requires positive aids with a good steady outside leg. The outside rein can be eased but not so much that contact is lost or the outside shoulder falls out. The inside rein guides the horse through the turn. The inside leg is on the girth.

Each turn needs a change of the rider's weight in the saddle, which is achieved by putting more weight on the inside stirrup and pushing forward onto the inside seatbone. The outside shoulder is taken forward a little in order to stay parallel with the horse's shoulders. The rider should be in a similar position to that when riding a bicycle, using the same actions and distribution of his body.

The young horse, to avoid bending, will try to go straight or move the inside hind leg sideways. For these reasons it is important to ride from the inside leg to the outside rein.

Aids for riding through a corner

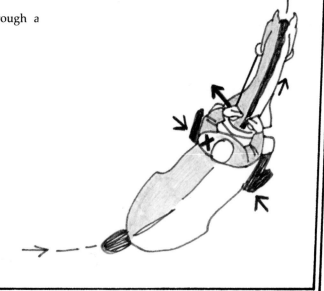

Working trot on the circle. Ruth Klimke with the 7-year-old Westfalian chestnut gelding "Feuerball" by "Fruhling"

RIDING ON A CIRCLE   To go correctly around a circle the horse must be continuously turning. That is why riding a circle is the logical follow up to riding through the corner. It is easier to ride a circle as the turn is not so sharp.

The young horse should not find it difficult to work on the circle as it learned to do so when being lunged. It is difficult, however, to achieve the correct bend through the body the circle and that needs careful training. The first thing is to correct the horse's natural crookedness, to straighten it, so we start work on the circle when we have straightened up a little of our horse's natural crookedness.

With lazy horses, in the early stages, I do not ride them on circles but in long lines to get them going. If a lazy horse is worked on a circle it loses its movement. I like to take such horses onto a racecourse to make them go forward until they feel like bucking. The opposite is needed with nervous horses, if one rides them in lines one must use hands, and start pulling which creates more tension and means they have to be ridden until they become tired. With such horses I use the circle and trick them into settling down. Such horses will not lose their movement on the circles as horses 71 which are fresh will not lose their gaits. Consequently it depends on the horses whether I do any circle work before straightening them a little. Once they have lost a little of their natural crookedness then they all start circle work.

I use the same aids on the circles, as those discussed for riding through the corner. They are also appropriate for riding 10 m voltes, half circles back to the track, turns and riding through corners.

RIDING LOOPS Riding loops in serpentines or off the track is a useful exercise to make the young horse obedient to the changing aids necessary for these movements. We start by riding a rather shallow loop along the long side in the walk. After that we ride it in working trot. We try to help the horse by changing our weight when changing the direction. This is of real importance when riding loops with a young horse. We need this lesson later on when riding across country or show jumping.

We do rising trot when practising loops. Before changing direction we establish a good contact with the reins and change the bend of the horse to the new direction. As the horse's education progresses we ask more of it, increasing the number of loops along the long side and the number of loops in the serpentines across the school.

Double loop on "Feuerball" on the long side changing from right to left

RIDING THE FIGURE OF EIGHT AND LARGE VOLTE When we have established the correct way to perform loops and serpentines we can progress to riding a volte (circle) of approximately 10 m and a figure of eight along the short side. We start by riding the volte in the corner of the school as that helps to prevent the outside shoulder falling out. We give the same aids as those for riding through the corner, but continue with them when coming out of the corner. The circle we ride can reach to the middle of the short side but later we make the circle smaller until it measures about 8 m. To make the horse bend equally well on both reins we ride the figure of eight on the short side. We change the bend of the horse as we practised in the serpentines. We can do two to three figure of eights during an hour's lesson but always follow them by going straight again.

Half-halts and halts

Having schooled our horse so that he accepts the forward aids, loops and serpentines and ridden leg yielding to teach him the lateral aids, we now round off the education by teaching him to accept the restraining aids. This is the most difficult part of the basic training. We made the first step in this direction when we put the horse on the bit and taught him to take hold of it. While doing this, the rider's hands remained passive to ensure a quiet head and neck carriage, and now we go a step further. We want to make the horse "durchlassig" and we have defined "durchlassig" as meaning the obedience of a horse which is already "losgelassen", to the forward, sideways and restraining aids.

The key to this is the halts. They are the proof that the horse is truly "durchlassig" and with such a horse we are in a position to be able to lengthen and shorten the horse's stride without any resistance. We differentiate between half-halts and halts. The halt is prepared by one or more half-halts regardless of the pace but according to the training of the horse. The purpose of the half-halt is to put the horse into a lower gear, to regulate the speed in any of the three paces and to shorten the latter. With further education the half-halts will improve the horse's carriage and rhythm and that is the beginning of collection. The half-halt is the most frequently used exercise in training.

The rider should make a half-halt every time he asks for a new movement, before he changes direction or changes the pace. The use of the half-halt is appropriate whenever the horse's attention is needed.

The half-halt should be used before: riding through a corner, a half pirouette at the walk, a circle, starting to trot or canter, riding over cavalletti or facing an obstacle. The function of the half-halt is to put the centre of gravity briefly further onto the hind legs, but this will only be achieved if the horse gives in the neck. Any resistance in the neck will simply result in interrupting the movement. We want to maintain the fluency of the movement and simply change the weight distribution so the horse comes into more collection. This is the secret which you see with my horses. In the

The aids for the half-halt are best when weight, leg and rein aids are given at the same time

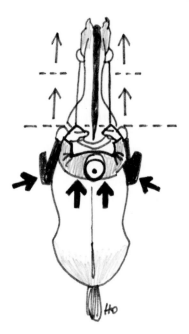

transitions they do not change the rhythm, they only change from a long stride to a more collected stride. To be able to do this there must be no stiffness in the hind quarters, back or in the neck or jaw. All these areas, if resistant, lead to an interruption of the movement and this is the biggest mistake in making half-halts. The secret of good transitions is the half-halt and to do this the whole horse must give. Showjumpers can just stop the movement with their half-halts, but for dressage the movement must be retained.

Good half-halts fulfil these conditions and are never painful for a horse, but a bad half-halt can be painful, and even painful to the spectator.

The more frequently a rider uses half-halts the easier it will be for the horse to shift its weight back and the lighter it will become in front and the more supple in its movements.

How do I teach the young horse the half-halt? Definitely not by pulling on the reins. The aids for a half-halt are a combination of weight, leg and hand. The rider sits deeper in the saddle and applies both legs, and at the same time pushes the horse into quiet receptive hands. The next moment the rider takes a hold with both hands but releases the hold immediately he feels that more weight has been put on the hind legs and the quarters are more engaged. That is the ideal case.

A useful exercise to establish the half-halt is from trot. Apply the restraining aids, but immediately the horse walks, apply the forward aids. In this way the horse learns without disturbing the movement in a pace. The transition to walk makes the horse change its weight and put more weight behind (part of collection) and when it is pushed smoothly forward again it will start to develop the "schwung". This is the right basis from which to establish "schwung" because through downward transitions the hind legs come under the horse and when they are there they can be used to trot forward and to develop better movement.

We must be prepared, however, for the half-halt not to be completely successful at first. It takes weeks and months for the horse to really understand the half-halt and to willingly accept it. The rider needs much experience and fine, sensitive feeling hands to balance the aids for the half-halt correctly. Too strong a seat can make the horse hollow its back against the rider as its muscles are not strong enough to accept the pressure without pain. Too strong a leg can possibly make the horse too heavy in the hand so that the rider misses the moment when the horse accepts the half-halt and it simply starts to pull. If, after the forward aid, the horse does not respect the rider's hands and starts leaning on the bit, the rider must ease the reins immediately and start the exercise again from the beginning. It is important that the rider's hand does not act as a support for the horse. The reactions of the rider must be quicker than those of the horse.

To begin with it must be rather confusing for the horse; the quick change of giving and taking the reins combined with the weight and leg aids and this can easily lead to some resistance. When the horse gives and accepts even a little of the half-halt it should be praised and the exercise stopped at once. After a short break we can repeat the exercise and when there is even a small success we praise the horse. The horse will thank us and reward us for our patience. This is one of the secrets of working with horses, that they will be more willing to follow our wishes when they realise that we appreciate them and that we have been patient and chosen the right moment to apply the lesson.

The more the half-halt improves during further education the greater is the rider's influence over the horse and the harmony between horse and rider. A pliable wrist is of decisive importance. As the education advances a deeper seat and closing of the fingers can be sufficient aid for the half-halt. This is hardly noticeable to the onlooker who only sees the change in the horse's carriage. Riding is then an art.

The halt is a continuation of the half-halt. If the transition is made from trot or canter one or two half-halts are given as preparation. The aids for half-halt and halt are the same. When the horse has halted, the rider must ease the reins and relax his hands. He has to be careful that the horse will stand still and bear its weight equally on all four legs. The rider then eases his weight in the saddle, sits straight, is ready with seat and leg to stop the horse from stepping back and, if necessary, makes the horse move one or the other hind leg to make it stand square.

As soon as the horse tries to stretch its neck, the rider's hand follows with a light contact to prevent any restlessness in the head and neck.

To begin with we should let the horse take its time before coming to a halt. Slowly we improve on this until we can halt at a prescribed point. We have then brought this exercise to its completion. In the first year of training we only ask for the halt out of walk and trot. The halt directly from canter is achieved at the end of the basic training. We only ask for that when the half-halt from canter to walk is securely established.

The rein back

The rein back helps to improve the obedience and "durchlassigkeit" of the horse. It is an unnatural movement for the horse which is why it is used as a punishment. The foot fall is diagonal as in the trot. We only start practising the rein back when the halt from walk and trot has been truly established. There has to be a certain degree of "durchlassigkeit". If the horse has not yet learned to shift its centre of gravity onto the hind legs in the halt he will not be able to understand the aids for the rein back. This does not mean that green horses cannot go backwards. After all, we see some young horses creeping backwards to avoid the rider's aids, but it is more normal for a young horse to avoid the aids by taking fright and lunging forwards.

To teach the young horse the rein back we need a combination of weight, leg and hand aids. To start with the horse must be straight and on the bit. We then give the same aids as for riding forward but at the moment the horse prepares to move forward the rider takes a stronger hold of the reins which makes it step backwards diagonally.

Some trainers recommend moving the reins from side to side, always to the diagonal hind which should step backwards. I think this a matter of taste, the disadvantage being it is easier for the horse to move sideways and avoid the rider. The leg should remain in contact with the horse in order to be in the position to correct it if necessary.

To make the rein back easier for the young horse, and especially one with a weak back, the rider should not sit heavily and should perhaps even lean a little forward. When introducing the rein back the first aids are therefore given almost only with the legs.

The aids for the rein back: (*left*) rider uses a relaxed back; (*right*) the rider with a light seat

Rein back. Lower leg behind the girth, a light seat and a restraining contact with the horse's mouth. The legs step diagonally

If a horse has real difficulties in reining back I have found the following method successful. I apply the aids as if I wanted the horse to do a turn on the fore hand but at the moment the horse lifts the inside hind leg I apply equal pressure on both reins and through that the horse goes backwards. The rein back may be a bit crooked but I have found it overcomes any resistance by the horse to move its hind legs.

In the more novice tests in Germany no definite number of steps are asked for in the rein back. We should not ask for more than four or five steps in a rein back otherwise it will be taken as a punishment. Do not let us forget: the exercise is not an end in itself, but a means to an end. We merely need the rein back to improve the horse's "durchlassigkeit" – no more – no less.

10 To Straighten the Natural Crookedness of the Horse

By this stage we have with patience made the horse more supple, interfered as little as possible with its natural rhythm and practised the aids for forward, lateral and restraining movements. We realise now that even with this build up in groundwork, we still have another problem to solve before we can truly develop the horse's paces and create "schwung". Before going any further we have to straighten the horse. The hind legs must follow those of the fore legs when going in a straight line. This is against the natural crookedness of the young horse.

It is usual for the right hind leg to come down to the outside. Horses are usually crooked from the right leg behind to the left leg in front. The result of this is that the horse resists against the rider's right leg and does not like to accept the right rein, it tries to find support on the left rein and falls on the left shoulder.

As the left hind leg is more strongly developed than the right, it is more natural for the horse to canter on the left leg and it is easier for him to support the weight on that leg. The conditions are the opposite if the horse is crooked the other way, but this rarely happens.

It is difficult to achieve straightness by riding in straight lines but may be possible as long as we do not interfere too much with the horse's action and do not try to engage the hind legs too much. The aids of the rider are as follows: the rider tries to guide the horse's fore hand to the right with the right rein, until the right fore hand is on the same track as the hind quarters. The right lower leg is applied behind the girth to push the right hind leg to the inside. The left lower leg is on the girth and asks the horse to go forward. The left hand is against the neck to stop the horse falling on the left shoulder. This exercise is really the beginning of the shoulder-in when ridden on the right rein. There is the danger however that the horse may lean even more on the left rein.

In my experience only systematic work on the circles and figures of eight can straighten a horse.

How do we proceed? A basic exercise which I have practised with success, is using diagonal aids on the circle.

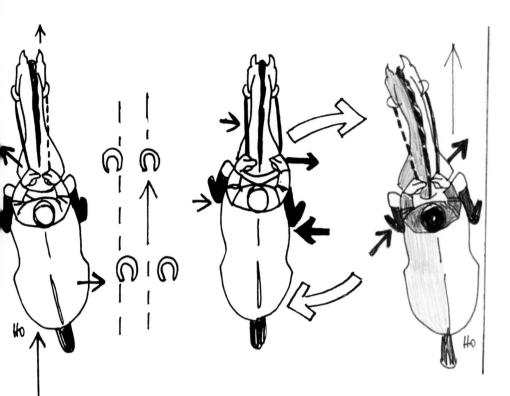

The natural crookedness of the horse: (*left*) it is usually the right hind leg that goes to the side, the horse leans on the left rein and falls on the left shoulder; (*centre*) correcting the natural crookedness on a straight line; (*right*) correcting the natural crookedness by riding the shoulder fore

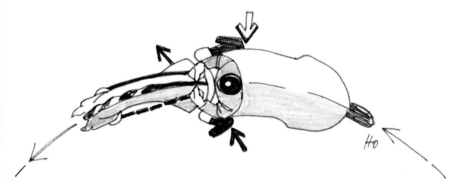

Correcting the natural crookedness by riding the shoulder fore

We ride in working trot on the left rein on a circle. The rider pushes the horse with the left inside leg, against the outside rein until the horse accepts and takes the outside rein and thoroughly relaxes to the inside left. We achieve a constant contact with the right rein and thereby put more weight on the right shoulder. The horse itself will be straight.

A similar exercise is a hint of a shoulder-in, known as shoulder fore, on the left rein on the long side with only a very slight bend of the neck. The inside hand gives as often as possible. The outside hand stays quiet. This will improve the acceptance of the right rein and thereby the straightening of the right hind leg. We can achieve the same effect by riding a slight shoulder-in on the circle. The diagonal aids are used and the fore hand brought to the inside of the circle.

Only when I have advanced to the point that I can straighten the horse with diagonal aids, does the work on the circle achieve its true significance. By using the circle we can put more weight on the inside hind leg and thereby make it more active. The degree of weight can be varied and increased by making the circle smaller until it is a volte (6 m in diameter). Voltes should only be ridden for short periods and the circle should be enlarged again soon and the horse asked to go forward into longer strides.

The uneven weight on the inside hind leg can lead to strain. We have to make sure that we do not lose the impulsion in the trot and shorten it. Our aim is to straighten the horse so that we can improve its carriage and lengthen its strides, but one cannot deny that the work on the circle with the aim of acceptance of the diagonal aids can restrict the "schwung" and the movements for the moment. We have to accept this small shortcoming if it means that we surmount the greater one, namely the crookedness. But we must realise we are doing it, and take even greater care to ride forward on straight lines and to lengthen the strides after riding the circles.

11 Development of the Three Paces

We have created the necessary conditions (hypothetically), now that the horse is "losgelassen" and moving with rhythm, is "durchlassig" and straight, to carry on and achieve our true objective of the training which is to improve its natural "schwung".

The only obstruction is whether or not the horse has any natural ability. We must not have any illusions – not every horse develops three good paces. This depends on the horse's conformation and its characteristics. Some horses lack the trot, others the canter or walk. A knowledgeable horseman can recognise this when he sees the horse loose. But a good horseman also knows what possibilities there are as to improving the paces. Through systematic training I have been successful with horses which were at first not at all promising. One can have pleasant surprises when working a horse correctly as long as the horse is willing to learn and temperamentally suited to do so.

Development of the trot

The trot is a movement in two time and a pace we use most during the basic training. This is the easiest of the paces as it is two time. We have four different trots: working, collected, medium and extended. During the basic training we make most use of the working and medium trot.

The working trot is the same as the natural trot except that one asks for a little more freshness to the movement, a little more animation and engagement of the hind quarters than would be natural. Through sympathetic forward aids the horse is encouraged to work.

That is the normal approach, but there are many horses, especially those with much thoroughbred blood, that are over active. With these, the rider must not push but sit quiet to let the horse move forward unconstrained and with rhythm. The tendency of the rider should be to slow down the horse and an aid to this is the use of cavallettis. In rising trot he lets the horse go over them in working trot.

When looking at the horse the hind feet should cover the tracks of the front feet (i.e. track up). It is difficult to develop the trot when riding in a group as the length of stride of each individual horse will differ. It is 81

82   Footfall in the trot

Young horse in balance in a working trot. Reiner Klimke on "Volt"

definitely better to ride singly. To establish the horse's pace, I do recommend riding in a group sometimes, with one horse following the other but with an experienced rider leading on a well-schooled horse.

The development of the trot is part of the schedule of the lessons. We start off by loosening up the horse, so that it is moving with rhythm and is "losgelassen". We then have a short break just walking on a loose rein. To start work we shorten up the reins bit by bit until we establish contact with the horse's mouth. We then trot on and put the horse on the bit as earlier described. Until this stage we have risen to the trot but now sit in order to be able to use our weight more positively. The rest of the work depends on the progress we have mapped out for that day. Sitting trot should not be used in the first few weeks of working a young horse. We wait until the muscles of his back are stronger. We also take care not to practise the medium trot too early. This is only added to our programme when the horse can hold itself in the sitting trot and accepts the half-halt. To begin with it is enough to increase the freshness of the strides from a natural to a working trot.

We can ask for a little more at the end of the lesson, when going along the long side in rising trot. We call this exercise "lengthened trot". The lengthening is created by a more active hind leg. We have to pay special attention at this stage to ensure that the steps do not become more hurried. If this happens we have to reduce the tempo (speed of the rhythm) with one or more half-halts and start again. We can repeat this several times to find out 83

"Lengthened trot" of a 4-year-old at the end of a lesson. Reiner Klimke on "Volt". A good position of the head and neck. Good "schwung" developing. The hind quarters not yet lowered enough

"Lengthened trot" of a young horse at the end of his basic training, which is approaching a medium trot. Reiner Klimke on the 5-year-old Oldenburger gelding "Notturno" by "Nachtflug". Excellent "schwung" with energetically engaged hind legs

"Releasing the reins", proof of the relaxed horse. Hans Jurgen Meyer on the 6-year-old Hanoverian gelding "Wallace" by "Wedekind"

whether the horse has misunderstood us or hurries because its muscles are not strong enough to allow the strides to lengthen. We have to take some risks to develop the trot in the way we mean it to be developed. The rider must feel how much or little he can ask.

We finish the lesson of lengthening with the gradual releasing of the reins exercise. (The literal translation of releasing the reins is to let the reins be champed out of the hands – "zugel-aus-der-hand-kanen-lassen".) We turn onto a circle, open our fingers and gradually let the horse take the reins through the hands. Every horse that has been on the bit for some time has the urge to stretch its tired neck muscles. The way the horse reacts to this tells us whether or not our work has been correct. If the horse stretches its neck with the nose forward and downwards, in other words relaxes and rounds its back, we can be satisfied. If it drops the head and does not try to stretch the neck forward we know the work was wrong. During the lesson 85 the rider had neglected to ride the horse forward onto the bit and the back of the horse remained stiff. The next day the rider will have to pay special attention to riding the horse forward onto the bit. Should the horse try to snatch the reins out of the hands this is an indication that the rider had pulled the reins with hands that were too strong.

After releasing the reins, we can either finish the lesson or, following a short break in the walk on a long rein, do some canter work.

MEDIUM TROT   Medium trot is the extension of the "lengthened trot" exercise. It is distinguished by longer swinging steps in a more extended frame.

The horse should stretch itself to cover more ground. The "schwung" is created by energetic bending and stretching of hips, knee joints and hocks. The action leads to the flow of movement "through" the horse's back to the front. The greater the "schwung" the more the horse will grow. The neck and head will be carried higher with the nose slightly in front of the vertical.

We are entering the field of more advanced dressage.

EXTENDED TROT   The development of the extended trot requires a higher degree of collection and education. It is logical not to practise the extended trot during the basic training of the young horse. I will describe the characteristics of the extended trot however so as to complete the picture: The extended trot is the ultimate forward movement in the trot. It shows the highest degree of activity and "schwung" and the highest influence of the rider's forward aids. We consider it a climax and end result of a well-planned and all-round gymnastic education of the horse.

COLLECTED TROT   The collected trot is another pace we do not develop in a young horse. Collection is started at the end of the basic training. It demands "losgelassenheit" and "durchlassigkeit". In the basic training we only need the beginning of collection which we establish with half-halts. It is most important when asking for a half-halt in the trot to give again immediately and urge the horse forward with seat and leg aids to keep the forward movement. This helps build up of muscles more than if we try to develop the collected trot by shortening the strides. In the collected trot the steps are higher, the strides shorter, the hind quarters lower and the neck and head carried higher.

Development of the canter

The canter is a jump-like movement in three time and is the faster pace of the horse. Depending on which pair of legs is leading, we have right canter or left canter. The footfall of the horse is in the three time. The fourth phase is the one of a short moment of suspension with all four legs of the horse in the air.

The footfall in the right canter

The sequence of the canter is as follows:
1. outside hind leg
2. inside hind leg and outside fore leg
3. inside fore leg
4. suspension

When galloping the second phase is not clear and a four time beat is heard.

In the canter we differentiate between the collected, working, medium and extended canter. Should the rhythm be lost in the canter, as it is sometimes in a wrongly shortened canter, then it is called a four time canter when the footfall is as follows:
1. outside hind leg
2. inside hind leg
3. outside fore leg
4. inside fore leg

The properly executed canter is distinguished by distinct three time hoof beats, a definite moment of suspension and "Schwung" needed to develop the definite canter step and makes it lively and natural.

The canter has not been dealt with in the previous chapters, as it should not be asked for until the young horse is truly accepting the rider's aids in the trot. We do not, of course, stop the horse from cantering if it feels like it, either in the arena or when hacking out. On the other hand it should not be forced to canter as most horses find it easier to carry themselves in the trot. We also have to make the horse familiar with the aids for canter otherwise it is apt to rush forward and we then have to correct it by pulling at the reins.

How does one canter on? A big circle is ridden in working trot and a half-halt asked for at the wall side of the circle. The rider then shifts his weight to the inside by pushing the inside hip forwards and putting more weight on the inside stirrups. The rider then puts the outside leg behind the girth and takes a light contact with the inside rein. He then asks for the canter by pushing the inside seatbone forwards in connection with a tightening of the back muscles and pressure with both legs (the inside on the girth, the outside behind the girth) and an easing of the inside rein. It would be wrong to canter for any length of time. There is a risk if the horse still has difficulty in balancing itself. We should therefore be satisfied with one or two rounds in the canter, stop the canter aids and let the horse fall into trot. When doing it for the first time we only ask for a few trot steps, then walk, let go of the reins and praise the horse, before collecting the reins starting to trot again and to repeat the strike off into canter. In later lessons we repeat the transitions from canter to trot several times. Use the whole school to encourage ground covering canter strides and apply strong driving aids to keep the horse going forward.

We must not be surprised if the young horse strikes off on the wrong leg sometimes. Most horses have a weaker and a stronger side. As a rule the young horse finds it easier to canter on the left leg, as its natural crookedness means that the left hind leg can support weight more easily than the right.

88

We therefore first use the diagonal aids to straighten the horse on its difficult side before asking for canter. We also check if we ourselves have given the correct aids or perhaps collapsed the hip.

As the education progresses we refine the canter aids and in the end we only have to use our seat to strike off. As the natural crookedness is generally more noticeable in the canter than in the trot the inside leg must be applied strongly as soon as the horse has struck off in the canter.

To canter for long does not improve the canter stride. The horse gets tired and loses its "schwung" and the hind quarters are dragged along. Experience shows that the best way to develop the canter is by frequent transitions on the circle between trot to canter. The horse is not advanced enough for us to use the half-halt to improve the canter. The breakthrough only occurs when the horse's "durchlassigkeit" has advanced to the point that one can practise the transitions directly from walk to canter and canter to walk. This establishes the canter work and helps us when riding across country and jumping.

Working canter on the gallop track in a beautiful balance. Ruth Klimke on "Optimist". Inside leg of the rider is a little far back

MEDIUM CANTER   When the horse is "losgelassen" and is in self carriage. in the working canter we can lengthen the strides on the long side to *medium canter*. Longer and more ground covering springy strides are asked for. The movement should not be flat but rather going uphill with lowered croup. This is normally only achieved when the rider uses the dressage seat. The canter can also be ridden with a light forward seat. This is used mainly out in the country when the horse is lower in front. This approach is recommended for strengthening the back muscles. In Germany, at the St Georg Riding Club of Munster, we have near the outdoor arenas a specially built gallop so that the horses can be given a canter on a straight line without any interference. It is my experience that the trot and canter strides are best improved when the lengthening and shortening can be practised on long straight lines. It will come more easily and naturally to the horse as it is closer to its natural movement.

EXTENDED CANTER   The extended canter can be ridden in the country with a light, forward seat. It is too early in the horse's education to develop further the riding of the extended canter.

COLLECTED CANTER   Similarly the *collected canter* should not be part of the programme in the basic training of the young horse. That will only be asked for in more advanced tests.

   To test whether the horse is in self carriage we like to use the exercise "stroking the horses neck" (uberstreichen). We can do this in the trot but

Development of the medium canter. A longer outline with longer strides "upwards". Reiner Klimke on the 7-year-old Trakehner grey gelding "Fabian" by "Donauwind"

Stroking the neck with both hands in canter. The position of the horse stays the same. Heinz Brüggemann on the Westfalian gelding "La Pace" by "Lugano"

should do it more in the canter. In the canter it is asked for in some tests. In this exercise both hands are moved forward "stroking the horse's neck" above the horse's mane so that temporarily there is no contact with the mouth. After a canter stride without contact the hands are taken slowly back to their original position and contact with the horse's mouth re-established.

Unsettled horses react well to this movement and quieten down if it is repeated a few times. The rider's seat stays unchanged. Only the hands move forward. The horse's nose should go forward a little but otherwise keeps its tempo, rhythm and outline. If these are maintained then the basic training is correct.

Finally we can find out whether the horse is on the outside rein. We move the inside hand forward and pat the neck. This action is not asked for in dressage tests. It is nevertheless useful when giving diagonal aids.

Development of the walk

The walk is a marching movement in four time. The footfall is in diagonal sequence with equal intervals between the hoofbeats. The sequences in the walk is:
1. Right fore foot
2. Left hind foot
3. Left fore foot
4. Right hind foot

92　The footfall in walk

Any deviation from this is incorrect; especially the pacing type of footfall when the four time rhythm is so hurried that phase 1 and 4 as well as 2 and 3 nearly happen together. We differentiate between the following walks: medium, extended and collected walk.

MEDIUM WALK The medium walk is a working pace. The horse strides out energetically, actively and regularly. There is slight overtracking (hind hoofprints slightly in front of fore hoofprints).

EXTENDED WALK In the extended walk the strides are lengthened as much as its conformation allows. Nevertheless they must not be hurried. The hind feet must track up well over the fore feet. The rider allows the horse full freedom of neck without losing contact with the mouth.

COLLECTED WALK In the collected walk the neck is higher and the height reached depends on the degree of collection. The strides are shortened and therefore there is no overtracking. The steps have more elevation as the joints are more flexed. The activity has to be maintained.

During the basic training it is only too easy to make mistakes with the walk. One can only talk of a development of this pace, as any trainer would be well advised with a young horse during its basic training to ride walk mainly on a long rein, or at the end of the lesson with a loose rein. I recommend this, as it is when walking on the bit that uneven strides develop which are extremely difficult to eradicate.

Why should we ask for more problems than necessary? My experience is that young horses which have learned to trot and canter on the bit will do this later on, also in the walk. I have not been able to reverse the above method with the horses that have come to me for training.

The most common fault with riders in the walk is that they use too strong a hand and even a restraining hand. I think the reason for this is that at the walk there is no "schwung" without the strong movements of the trot and canter, the rider is unconscious of not using enough leg to the amount of hand. For these reasons I cannot approve of the method of training which puts the horse on the bit, first in the walk, before the trot and canter. I prefer to follow the principle: when the horse is securely on the bit in trot and canter, he will achieve the same in the walk. I do not have to practise walking on the bit.

During a horse's basic training I let him walk freely on a loose rein as much as possible. I forget about the extended and collected walk at this stage. I use the medium walk when practising transitions from walk to trot, and vice versa; and from canter to walk, and vice versa; as well as for leg yielding and riding circles and figures in the arena. Some may say that I am avoiding the issue with this method. I also understand that some experienced trainers, such as Watjen, have different ideas and ask the young horse to go on the bit in medium walk and trot before cantering. I can only continue to support what experience has taught me and what I have practised. I preach riding 93

Walk on a loose rein with a happy horse. Irena Meyer on the 4-year-old Westfalian stallion "Poseidon" by "Paradox"

with a long rein in the walk as it will reduce the number of faults created by the hands of an inexperienced trainer.

I warn against exercising too long in the walk especially with a horse which is not straight (which most young horses are not), because it becomes natural to step unevenly, the legs do not come "through" enough because it does not understand the leg aids. The result is an uneven walk. The danger is smaller with a trained horse because then the aids come "through" and the horse will follow my leg aids.

In the basic training we only ride two sorts of walk: the free walk and the medium walk. In the first year of training we ride the free walk with a long rein. In the second year we develop the medium walk, first when out hacking, then in the school during the transitions leg yielding and figures. Those riders who are brave and are talented enough to feel any unlevelness could practise the medium walk on the bit.

12 Tips for the Training of Horses with Difficult Temperaments and Faulty Conformation

The breeding of horses has made great advances in the last twenty years. The riding horses now available are on the whole of a greatly improved quality. In spite of this we know that there is no such thing as a horse without faults. We all wish for the perfect horse but it is very rare that we find one. The art of training is to recognise the potential of the horse and to develop it to the utmost. We must know how and to what extent we can eliminate faults in temperament and conformation. This needs considerable experience which can only be gained by handling different horses over the years.

It has to be realised that although the training of each horse is different and individual to it, this still lies within the framework of the methods laid down in the previous chapters. There are methods, however, which will be of help when dealing with difficult temperament and defective conformation. This does not mean that the basic training as such is abandoned but rather rounded off and it remains in spite of the problem.

Difficult temperaments

The horse is born with its temperament and physique. We can improve both with the right education and environment making it possible to use the horse for riding. On the other hand, the reverse can happen if wrong and bad handling is practised. The faults with which the horse is born, and acquires, are difficult to correct. Experience teaches that even after patient and hard work faults can reappear in a horse when an opportunity presents itself.

NERVOUS HORSES   Nervous horses are inclined to take flight when faced with unusual situations such as strange noises, quick movements and flags. These horses can be calmed down with much careful work and patience. It becomes more difficult if the horse is also nervous of the going or of objects   95 on the ground. It is my experience that a horse with this characteristic will never completely lose its nervousness. The trainer just has to accept the limitations. In contrast, a certain excessive sensitivity and nervousness can be used to advantage. I personally prefer to train a lively horse, even if it is a bit nervous and anxious, rather than a lazy one. The nervous horse is grateful to the rider who sits quietly, hardly moves and can wait. It needs fewer aids as long as the rider is patient and uses waiting aids; the day will come when the horse accepts the leg and can be ridden forward. Then one has won but a rider with limited patience should never ride a nervous horse.

LAZY HORSES   Lazy horses can drive the rider to distraction. First of all we should find out whether the horse is naturally lazy or if there is any other reason: for example, it may not be fit enough, it may be ill or be ignorant of the rider's aids. It is best to take a lazy horse out into the country, preferably with a forward going companion. If the idleness persists, the rider can take stronger action. At the right moment he uses short sharp applications of the whip. If the horse then jumps forward it should be praised immediately. In my experience this method has to be repeated a few times before the horse realises what is required of it and subsequently reacts to much lighter aids. It is important that the rider carries this through to get the horse going forward. He must, and can then reduce the strength of his aids so that the horse does not become dead to them.

OBSTINATE HORSES   Obstinate horses can develop considerable strength and energy when they do not wish to submit to the rider. This is especially the case when they realise that the rider is not sufficiently strong and determined. This can quickly lead to the horse rearing which is a very unpleasant trait and difficult to cure. To correct this unpleasant habit, a brave rider is needed who sits firmly in the saddle and makes the horse go forward, without giving it a chance to be disobedient. When the horse obeys, the rider must be ready to praise it and re-establish the horse's trust. When the rider feels that the horse is about to rear or take off, a quick pull on one rein can prevent this disobedience but only apply it quickly and not for too long otherwise the horse could overturn with the rider.

Faulty conformation

Horses with a prominent fault in their conformation are rarely offered for sale as riding horses these days. If the fault is not too great it is a question of saving the weaker limbs and joints from doing too much and gradually building them up to the same strength as the rest of the horse. This is easier said than done.

FAULTY NECKS   These are rarely offered for sale these days but if in addition to these faults, the horse has a heavy, thick lower jaw the chances are slim of a true correction. A thick lower jaw makes it physically impossible

Faulty necks: (*left*) horse with swan neck; (*right*) horse with strong muscles under the neck (ewe neck)

for the horse to give easily in the neck as the lower jawbone presses against the neck and therefore obstructs it. I advise against schooling such a horse as a riding horse.

Faults of the neck, such as a broken neck (the poll not the highest point), are sometimes caused by too strong hands. When training young horses as well as correcting badly ridden horses we must adhere to the principle that those who want to change the neck of a horse must work the hind quarters and back.

A long thin neck which has a strong bend at the top and joins the wither at a high point is called a "swan neck". Horses with swan necks usually have difficulties in establishing a contact. We have to make a special effort to ride the horse for some time long and deep. They must not come up too early otherwise it could easily become a broken neck. Only when the horse has learned to stretch its neck forward and down, and is looking for the bit, can we continue with the training. If horses with "swan necks" are asked too early for a high head carriage they will often stay "wobbley" at the wither. The neck is not rigid, it can be pulled in or moved sideways, which can create dislocation of the neck and the outside shoulder falling out. It is especially important to ride horses with swan necks actively forward. Should the horse not take the bit I recomend trying a thicker snaffle. When riding through turns stronger outside aids are advisable. The fault can only be eradicated by strengthening the lower neck muscles through riding forward with the neck long and low.

''EWENECK'' This condition is seen when the lower muscles of the neck have noticeably developed. This makes it difficult for the horse to stretch its 97 neck. We must try to loosen the lower neck muscles and develop the top ones. It can be useful to ride the horse with low side reins or a third rein. A eweneck usually goes with a stiff back. Work over cavalletti is very helpful for loosening the back, and this is fully described in the next chapter. Also gymnastic jumping can be used.

FAULTY BACKS Horses with this problem do not always have to be problem horses. A *long backed horse* is often a more comfortable ride. If its back is well muscled up between wither and loin, its back cannot be called faulty. It is rather the opposite as a long supple back helps in the training. However, if the back is so long that the hind legs cannot reach the centre of gravity, then this is very difficult for dressage as the steps of the hind legs are too short. This fault may not be so serious for a showjumper or eventer as when making a mistake such a horse can use its back as a balancing pole. For dressage its use is limited as such a horse cannot overtrack and will never do well in tests. We must realise this when we start training such a horse. We cannot change a long back with training. We only have one chance: to encourage longer strides by repeated transitions and half-halts.

Horse with a long back and long second thigh

SHORT BACKS Such horses are, of course, easier to collect, as their hind legs come under more easily. On the other hand they often have back problems. The short back is usually rather tight and needs a comparatively long neck to relax it. If this is not forthcoming it is practically impossible to obtain ground covering strides. Short backed horses are not usually comfortable to ride. They can only be brought to their full potential when the rider pays special attention to loosening exercises and works with exceptionally light hands.

Horse with short back

HIGHER HIND QUARTERS   As they are not yet fully grown, young horses often have higher hind quarters than their wither. As a result of this more weight is put on the fore hand. If the young horse does not grow out of this it is unsuitable for dressage. It is not necessarily a fault for jumping, as shown by Olympic god medallist H. G. Winker's horse, Halla and Alfous Lutke-Westhue's horse, Ala.

A horse with higher hind quarters should not be ridden long and low for any length of time. Even during the loosening up period it should be asked to carry its head a bit higher to get it balanced.

Horse with higher hind quarters than withers

SICKLE HOCKS Horses with quarters which fall away often have "sickle hocks". As the hock angle is so small they cannot develop such strong and active action behind. This makes them unsuitable for jumping and one also has to be careful as to their use for dressage. It is true that such a horse can bring its hind legs well under its body but this puts additional strain on its back which can cause trouble. They should be ridden actively forward with only a little collection.

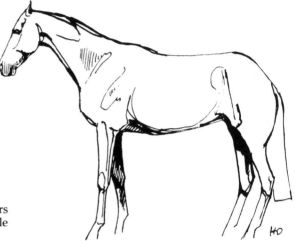

Horse with hind quarters which fall away and sickle hind legs

Hind leg faults: (*right*) horse with bowed shaped hind legs; (*far right*) horse with cow hocks

FAULTS IN THE HIND LEGS   These horses should be trained with caution. The trainer has to be quite clear in his mind how he can go with such horses. A so-called "cow hocked" horse (when the hind legs are too close together) provides the same danger as one with "bowed shaped" legs (hind legs far apart) as too much pressure is put on the hocks. Both types can only take limited collected exercises. In my experience more work can be done with the cow hocked horse than the other as the wear and tear on the latter is greater. One can try to establish balance with shoulder-in and diagonal aids. It is difficult to know however whether this will have lasting success.

It is only worthwhile to take the trouble to try and eliminate faults of temperament and conformation when there are other advantages.

13 Cavalletti Work

We have to thank the Italians for the invention of cavalletti. It was Caprilli who started using cavalletti when he changed the style of jumping at the turn of the century. He let his horses work over them in all paces, with or without a rider. He developed the work over cavalletti, which was adopted by the German cavalry schools as well as by the Italian. Cavalletti are an important aid when schooling young riding horses. I would not want to do without them when schooling horses and have had over thirty years experience in their use.

Why is it worthwhile to use cavalletti for the basic training of young horses? We must consider our aim again: to systematically train the young horse which has not been backed, or only just been backed, to carry the rider happily on its back in balance and to give the horse a posture and shape which will be a basis for future development of its capability. As well as this, the work should be varied and enjoyed by the horse so it does not get bored.

Correct work over cavalletti helps us in these aims. It serves to loosen up and strengthen the muscles, prepares for work over uneven ground and is a preparation for jumping. The young horse learns to move its centre of gravity quickly and confidently. It moves with more confidence once it has learned to step over the cavalletti. The muscles of the back will be strengthened due to having gone over cavalletti with a low head and neck. The horse learns to "dive", which means to lower its head and neck forward and downward as it approaches the jumps to find the best take-off point.

The cavalletti will help us to obtain an idea of the horse's peculiarities and enable us to act accordingly. The way a horse tackles the demands made by the cavalletti, whether it stays quiet and willing or bolts or refuses, enables us to draw conclusions about its temperament and character. By changing the distances and layout of the cavalletti we can assess and further the horse's natural ability. The horse becomes more attentive and learns to solve some problems for itself giving us many possibilities as to what we can teach the young horse during its basic training with the help of cavalletti.

In my book *Cavalletti* I have described the best way to use them and also pointed out the danger of their incorrect use. Anyone who would like to learn more about cavalletti will find it there. In this book I confine myself to cavalletti work for the basic training of the young horse.

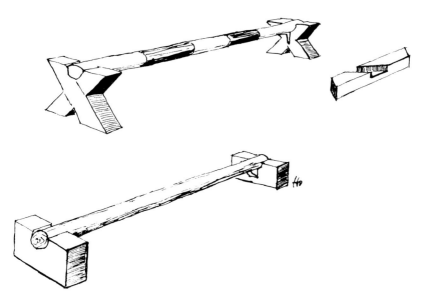

Different types of cavalletti

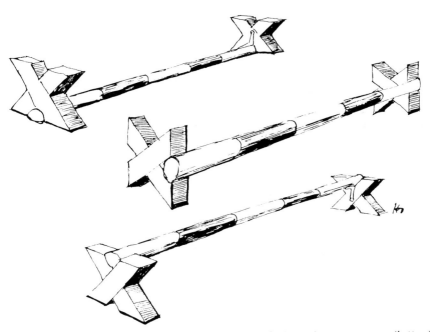

Cavalletti at different heights: (*top*) 15 cm–20 cm high; (*centre*) 20 cm–35 cm; (*bottom*) 50 cm.

Various types

There are different types of cavalletti but most are supported by a cross. The poles should be strong, thick and round so that the horse will respect them, and are less likely to break and splinter which could injure the horse. The best length is 2 m to 3 m because if the poles are too long it makes it more difficult for the trainer to ride the horse straight over them.

I prefer cavalletti with cross-ends. They are lighter and easier to move above. At its lowest, the pole is 15 cm to 20 cm off the ground. This is used especially for walk and trot work. For canter the pole should be about 50 cm off the ground, so that a true canter stride is developed and the horse learns to pay attention.

Poles as an alternative

If no cavalletti are available simple poles can be used. Poles as such have several disadvantages and are therefore in the strictest sense not a reasonable alternative. They do not reach to the minimum required height of 15 cm to 20 cm and the horses therefore do not pay proper attention to them. They are also more easily knocked by the horse and could be dangerous if the horse treads on them because they will roll. If this happens the horse could twist a fetlock or sprain a tendon. If poles are used instead of cavalletti one should make certain that they are fixed.

It is enough usually to have four to six cavalletti, or poles, at one's disposal. When schooling young horses it pays to put up wings or poles.

Ground conditions

The state of the going is of great importance but sadly is often neglected. The degree of work asked of the horse does not only depend on the number of cavalletti and the length of the exercise but, to a large extent. on the condition of the going.

Deep going makes it harder work, but has the advantage of give in the ground. Hard ground does not give and increases the danger of injury when poles are hit. We have to think about this if we want our work with cavalletti to be successful. If the choice lies between grass or sand, the latter is preferable as it is less slippery especially when damp. In any case, care must be taken that cavalletti are placed on level ground and that there are no holes in the ground.

Cavalletti work without a rider

It is easier for the horse to work over cavalletti without a rider. The horse is freer and less restricted without the weight of the rider and the interference from hand and spurs used at the wrong moment.

Those who have a small indoor school should continue loose schooling the young horse, but now add trot work over cavalletti. This should only be attempted after the young horse's education has reached the point where it happily accepts the rider's weight. We must not confuse the horse at the beginning of its schooling. It must first become used to the bridle, saddle and any other tack needed for riding. Concentrate on mounting and riding as described previously. Only after this introduce cavalletti and small jumps in furtherance of our basic training. If done too early, before the horse has learned to carry the rider without constraint, it would only cause worry. Do not then get cross if the young horse gets anxious and worried about the cavalletti instead of accepting them with confidence and pleasure. To repeat: *only* include cavalletti work after the horse has been ridden.

TROTTING OVER CAVALLETTI WITHOUT A RIDER   The cavalletti are put up but before using them let the horse move freely in the school as described earlier. Only then start trotting over cavalletti.

It is advisable to start off with one cavalletti and gradually increase it to four. When two cavalletti are put up the horse often mistakes it for a spread jump and tries to jump it in one. Therefore, when only two cavalletti are put down it is advisable to double the distance between them. Three or four cavalletti are best for trot work and this stage should therefore be reached quite soon. We put the cavalletti at their lowest, 15 cm to 20 cm height.

It depends on the horse's temperament and stage of education whether four cavalletti are used in the first lesson. Under no circumstances should more than four cavalletti be used at this stage in order to avoid any risk of asking too much of the horse. The best results are achieved if the work is a pleasure which is willingly carried out by the horse.

The trot distances between the cavalletti are 1·30 m to 1·50 m. The right distance to begin with is 1·30 m. After watching the horse over 1·30 m it may have to be altered and made suitable to the horse's trot strides. We start off working on the horse's favourite rein. It is perhaps asking too much to expect the young horse to trot willingly over the cavalletti when first introduced to them. It is usual for the horse to canter because it is worried and wants to get over the cavalletti as quickly as possible. This can look rather dangerous but in fact is not so. One has to leave the horse alone and let it settle until it starts trotting on its own. A few quiet words are the only help needed at this stage.

The placement of cones and wings will stop it from running out. If the horse should stop or turn round it is best to lead it to the cavalletti at the trot and then let go just in front of them. To begin with the horse could be led over the cavalletti.

When the horse is settled and trots quietly the work can begin. The trainer should now try to regulate the tempo of the trot. We know that as soon as a horse settles it becomes lazy so we have to encourage it by using our voice, clicking or lifting the lunge whip. One thing to watch out for is that the horse does not put in two small strides instead of maintaining an even rhythm.

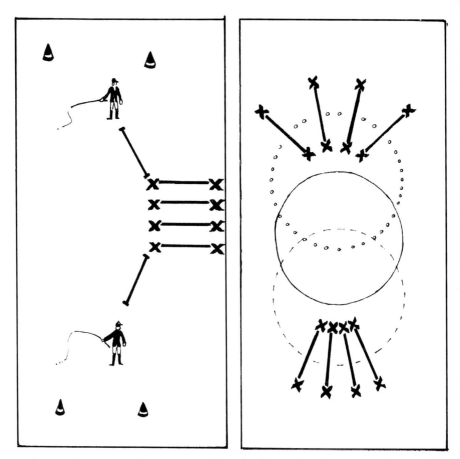

Using cavalletti. Note the wings or poles – useful in schooling a young horse: (*left*) cavalletti for loose schooling a horse; (*right*) cavalletti for lungeing, (*top*) 1 m for trot and (*bottom*) 0·80 cm for walk

Sensitive horses need little encouragement. Some, on the other hand, need a great deal. All horses are different. The quiet and understanding trainer will not have many difficulties in achieving a close contact with his horse. Those who still find this difficult will have the opportunity now to gain experience for the future.

The duration of this exercise depends on the stage of the horse's training. In my experience 10 minutes is sufficient especially as 10 to 20 minutes loosening up exercises have preceded the cavalletti work. Side reins can be used and how to put these on has been described earlier. In any case after 10 minutes the horse should walk out, the side reins taken off so that the movement of the horse's hind legs will not be restricted. Depending on the horse's fitness there could be another short trot period of 5 to 10 minutes.

The distances between the cavalletti should be carefully lengthened now to encourage longer trot steps. A medium trot should be asked for along the long side without cavalletti and working along the short side. This to be repeated a few times. Only then should the distances be increased. This must be done carefully so as not to lengthen its strides until it is in medium trot. How much the distances should be increased depends on the horse. The maximum is 1.50 m but this is too long if the horse has to put in small strides.

The lesson in which the lengthening of the stride has been asked for should come to an end after 5 to 10 minutes. The horse should now be allowed to walk around until it has dried off and is breathing steadily. Only then should the horse be taken back to the stable.

The question may now arise as to why I do not canter the horse over the cavalletti. The answer is that to canter over cavalletti needs power and is used for schooling jumpers and eventers. I discuss this in more detail later. Quite apart from this a lot more power is needed to canter over cavalletti and if this work follows the trotting over cavalletti it can overtax the horse. The work as described above has the aim of improving the trot and is complete in itself.

I have not found it beneficial to walk over the cavalletti. I am against using side reins at the walk as it can upset the overtracking and unevenness in the rhythm can creep in, but it is difficult to keep the horse on the track without side reins. Also without side reins any work is of little value as the use of the back cannot be properly controlled.

It only remains to ask how often this work should be carried out. Those who are able to ride their horses every day should let them trot loose over cavalletti every 8 to 14 days. I personally do not ride my horses on those days but use their "day offs" for this and to give them a change. Even if the horse is not regularly ridden the odd day of loose trotting over cavalletti is beneficial.

The use of the cavalletti for the basic training is recommended even if it cannot be carried out on a regular basis. It does not have, of course, quite the same value as when it is done as a routine.

WORK WITH CAVALLETTI ON THE LUNGE   The advantage of working the horse on the lunge over cavalletti is that it is possible to correct one sided stiffness. By putting the horse on a circle, it has to bend to the inside to follow the circle which makes it stretch the muscles on the outside of its neck and body. The inner hind leg carries more weight and has to therefore come more underneath the horse's body. The length of the strides can be varied by enlarging or making the circle smaller without moving the cavalletti. This has the advantage that after lengthening the strides the horse can re-establish the normal length of stride in the working trot.

It has to be said, however, that lungeing over cavalletti presents its difficulties. If one is not careful it is easy for the lunge rein to become entangled in the cavalletti. It is important to keep the circle absolutely round   107 as the space between the cavalletti varies from the inside to the outside. The trainer has to watch carefully all the time. I therefore recommend beginners to let their horse go free over cavalletti or perhaps ride them and only later lunge them. It is only easy to lunge when just one cavalletti is used.

ERECTING CAVALLETTI   For lungeing this is simple: one puts one end of the cavalletti on the track. When other horses are in the school it is best to put them on the open side of the circle so as not to disturb the horses one is working with. If someone wants to do just a little cavalletti work before riding his horse three or four cavalletti distributed around the circle are enough. This will keep the horse's attention while going on the circle.

When the cavalletti are used for the actual basic training of the paces I have found the most advantageous way to put them up is so they will not have to be moved during the lesson, although one has presumed that the horse has worked previously over cavalletti and can therefore negotiate several at a time. The middle circle serves for lungeing without cavalletti. The top circle is for the trot work and the lower one for the walk. The two open rides should be enclosed with wings or poles.

If eight cavalletti are not available, six will do but perhaps a pole could be placed between the cavalletti. These are perfectly adequate though it is important to ensure that they are fanned out to keep the rhythm of the circle going.

The distance for the trot poles is 1·30 m in the centre so that there is plenty of room for lengthening or shortening of the trot steps. The lowest height of 15 cm to 20 cm is sufficient. The distance in the centre for the walk circle should be 80 cm.

I do not recommend the use of cavalletti in the canter. The danger of injury is too great compared to the possible advantages, but I think it is a good idea to let horses canter over some small jumps. This, however, does not belong to the work over cavalletti but is part of the training for jumping. The reasons I was against walking when loose over cavalletti does not apply on the lunge, as the pace can now be more easily controlled and the horse kept active through the nearness of the trainer, and the whip.

LUNGEING WITHOUT CAVALLETTI   There has to be preparation before lungeing over cavalletti. The horse trots and canters on the middle circle for 5 to 10 minutes. The side reins are kept very long so as to just keep a light contact, or no side reins at all with an experienced horse. One must always remember that horses have one hour's work a day and spend twenty-three hours in the stable. That is why for the first few minutes it is nice for them to have some freedom without too much interference. Most horses will go happily around, some perhaps even rush around. A few calming words are then needed to settle the horse and get it going quietly. Giving and taking of the lunge rein will help and it is best to keep the whip under one's arm. There are some horses that have to be pushed at the beginning.

Putting on side reins

After lungeing on both reins the side reins are put on. One must remember that the horse will be going on a circle, so that the inner rein should be shorter than the outside one. The correct difference is between 5 cm and 8 cm, about 3 to 5 holes. The function of the reins is to prevent the horse from bending too much to the inside and falling out on to the outside shoulder. The outside rein has to be in contact. The side reins are put on as before, on the left and the right of the girth just below the saddle flap. This gives the horse freedom to stretch its neck forward and downwards.

The length of the reins should correspond with the length of the side reins and be adjusted when necessary. When the side reins are adjusted the horse is then asked to go on the centre circle for a few rounds in trot and canter, asking the horse to stretch its head and neck by the gentle use of the whip and an encouraging voice. The horse will be content to take the bit. To achieve this should take 10 to 15 minutes. When this work is over the cavalletti work can proceed. We have a short break just walking, and ask some kind person to help us put up the cavalletti.

LUNGEING OVER CAVALLETTI   The first thing is to get the young horse used to cavalletti. We start off with just one and let him go over it whichever way he likes. When he has settled down we add them until we reach the number as described before. It is best to start with the trot as the horse finds this the easiest pace, then finish with the walk. During a short pause, the horse can be praised and the side reins changed to work on the new rein. The walk can be continued and the horse asked to work over more cavalletti. Horses that are already used to cavalletti can benefit from varying the way they are erected.

After the horse has been lunged on the centre circle, it should be moved to one of the outside ones. There a difficulty arises straight away. It is important to get the horse to trot over the centre of the cavalletti so that the distances are correct. If it is brought in wrongly it will lose its confidence and the trainer will have trouble in getting it to trot quietly and in a relaxed manner over the cavalletti.

How do I enlarge the circle? By lengthening the lunge line and pointing the whip in the direction of the horse's shoulder. In addition the lunge line could be moved up and down in a snake like fashion to drive the horse to the outside. Increasing the circle should be practised a few times on the centre circle before going to the outer one with the cavalletti. Only then should the trot work begin over the cavalletti.

One has to realise that the inner hind foot will be put under special strain. The movements of the horse therefore must be carefully observed. Uneven strides after going over the cavalletti points to tension and perhaps even muscle pain. One should then go straight back to the centre circle. Even without this I recommend going back to the centre circle after trotting five to eight times over the cavalletti. After a few rounds in the centre go back to the outside. The constant change from one circle to the other is what helps to make the horse supple and work the muscles. Boring work makes the horse lose pleasure in its movements and all of riding is dependent on that.

Although the horse may be especially stiff on one side, one must not forget to change the rein. My experience is that horses relax quickly when the rein is changed frequently and are not continuously worked on the difficult side. The outside of the cavalletti circle should only be used when the trainer/rider has gained sufficient experience and dexterity. The contact between horse and trainer will improve in time with proper handling. The horse will need less and less help and one will be astonished to see how easily the horse can be guided when it has gained complete confidence. Only then will there be real pleasure in the work and a great basis for future riding.

The time for lungeing over cavalletti should not exceed 20 minutes, so that a lesson looks something like this: 5 to 10 minutes without the side reins; 10 to 15 minutes with side reins but without cavalletti, and 20 minutes in trot and walk over cavalletti; to finish, the horse is walked dry without side reins before going back into the stable.

This lesson should not be done more often than every 8 to 14 days, as the riding over cavalletti will have to be included in the training and more would put too much strain onto the young horse.

Cavalletti work with a rider

During the basic training we use cavalletti on their own or in combination with small jumps according to the aim of the lesson. When using the cavalletti with the aim of dressage, I have found several different ways of putting them up has proved successful depending on whether I want to ride over them in a straight line or in circles. For work in a straight line it is best to put the cavalletti just inside the track on the long side of the arena. This makes it unnecessary to ride over them on each round and gives the helper a chance to change them while the rider keeps going round. Wings could be put up to make things easier.

CAVALLETTI WORK IN WALK   To start a horse off over cavalletti it is best to do so in walk as that is the easiest pace to ride. To start with, only one cavalletti is used and it is ridden over on a completely loose rein. The amount of driving aids depend on how active is the horse. The first attempt has to be made at an active pace, perhaps with the aid of the voice. At the second attempt the horse usually pulls on its own and does not need much urging. The upper part of the rider's body should be slightly forward so that the rider does not restrict the horse's back.

If the horse remains quiet a second cavalletti can now be put up at a distance of 80 cm to 1 m. Shortly after that a third, fourth and so on, but not more than six. It is noticeable that horses get nervous when confronted by many cavalletti. Where this is the case, I usually have one or two removed

Cavalletti work in walk on a long rein. "Volt" ridden by David Pincus. Careful steps with pricked ears in good balance

until the horse settles down again. In some cases an increase in the number of cavalletti is too sudden. Removing some generally means that after a few minutes it is possible to put the additional cavalletti up again.

If the horse is used to cavalletti the complete number can be used straight away. If possible, it is best to have the reins loose for the first few times. This gives the horse a chance to find its own balance. If the horse keeps a constant rhythm, the distance between the cavalletti is correct, if not they have to be altered. This helps to develop the natural footfall of the walk. To do this exercise at the beginning of a lesson is a very good way of loosening the horse. The special value of this lesson is just that, and to settle it at the end of the lesson when it is drying off. In addition, through the proper influence of the rider the lengthening of the stride and the activity of the back can be improved. To achieve this we ride the horse on the bit in medium walk towards the cavalletti. The hands are preferably low. When within one horse length of the cavalletti the rider moves his hands forward so that the horse does not feel at all restricted. His upper body is tipped slightly forward to ease the weight of the horse's back. Correctly executed, the horse steps over the cavalletti with its head and neck low and back relaxed.

It is not always possible to maintain a light contact with the horse's mouth. Some horses stiffen up and go against the bit. In this, or similar cases, a suitable correction can be achieved by riding a volte or figure of eight

111

attempting to get the horse to give by careful aids. Then ride out of the circle towards the cavalletti and let the rein go long just before and over the cavalletti. Usually the horse will be happy to relax and stretch its neck and lower its head to see where it is going and thereby get rid of the tension in its back. The horse should be patted with the inside hand everytime if it has done the exercise properly. When it has been done correctly, the exercise can be repeated a few times more.

The most important points the rider has to watch out for are:

1. To ride straight.
2. To ride forward.
3. Low, long neck with only slight rein contact and low hands.
4. Co-ordination of the upper body with the horse's movements.

To approach the cavalletti crookedly and not riding straight over them interrupts the horse's rhythm as the distances are different and are longer when not on a straight line. To go slowly does not teach the horse to move its legs actively. The opposite is the fixed hand, in conjunction with a stiff upper body which interferes with the horse's back movement. I recommend the rider not to sit too deep before going over the cavalletti as it is then not usually possible to move the body forward when going over them. To encourage the horse on, it is best to use voice and lower leg. If a whip is carried it is best to use it on the horse's shoulder as it might make the rider lean back if used behind the saddle or on the croup.

The length of the walk stride can be improved by slowly lengthening the distance between the cavalletti. This exercise should be part of the lesson as only when the horse's back is relaxed can the full potential of its movements be developed. The lengthening of the distances depends on the size of the horse, anything between 0·80 m to 1·00 m to 1·10 m. As soon as the horse puts in short steps then it is a sign that the distances are too long. It could, of course, also be that the horse is lazy. The rider should feel this and push it a bit harder next time and should not let go of the reins until the horse is going over the first cavalletti, thereby giving it the full possibility of using itself. Because of the strain on muscles, tendons and ligaments the exercise "extended walk over the cavalletti" should not be repeated more than ten to fifteen times.

WORK OVER THE CAVALLETTI AT THE TROT   Those who have started cavalletti work in the walk as described above, will now be ready to trot straight away over several cavalletti. Those who start off in trot should only advance slowly from one to four cavalletti. The distances between them are now 1·30 m to 1·50 m. They are kept at the lowest height of 15 cm to 20 cm.

Trotting over cavalletti at the rising trot with a long, low neck has proved itself as a useful exercise for loosening up the horse. It is especially useful for strengthening and loosening the back muscles of the horse. It must be said that it is not easy for every horse to trot over cavalletti with a low head carriage. The reason for this is that there are no perfect horses in conformation or temperament. We must try to overcome these faults with training. A typical fault is the increase of speed on approaching the cavalletti. We do not have this problem if the horse is lazy, though most horses speed up when they see cavalletti and would really like to canter over them. The rider has to try and prevent this with half-halts and by giving and taking of the rein so that the horse does not lean on the bit. If the attempt to settle the horse does not succeed, the rider has to go back to just one cavalletti. If the horse has its nose in the air, it stiffens up, loses balance and can hurt itself by tripping up and slipping. There are a number of horses who like to raise their head when approaching a jump so that they can see it better. When going over the jump or cavalletti their head drops down naturally and their back rounds. It would be quite wrong for the rider to try and bring the horse's head down in this situation. It just creates resistance and the horse would soon lose confidence in its rider. On the other hand it could be that the horse has problems with its neck, a sensitive back or distrusts the bit. These horses are difficult to put on the bit, even without cavalletti. To get them to give, they should first be ridden on circles, volte and serpentines. Only when we have succeeded in stretching and carrying their neck low and keeping the same tempo can we start trotting over cavalletti.

It often helps to settle the horse by riding towards cavalletti and then turn away, ride a volte in front of the cavalletti, halt and rein back.

These are just suggestions and the rider has to decide when and how often to do these exercises. Every horse is different and the rider has to prove to himself that he has the patience and nerve to do it.

Cavalletti in rising trot. Careful steps with good neck position and light rein contact. David Pincus on "Volt"

Work over cavalletti to lengthen the trot strides

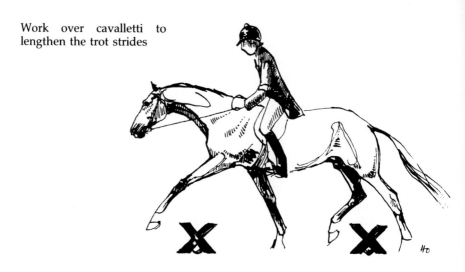

When a contact has been established and one has been successful once or twice, the rider will be quite surprised how happy the horse will be to trot over the cavalletti. After a few lessons the horse will be relaxed and will show no special excitement. The loosening effect of the cavalletti will help to overcome problems. If the horse gets excited again later on, this is proof that the rider has been careless with his preparation. If perhaps the horse has a pain somewhere and feels that too much is being asked of him, the work should be stopped immediately. The rules the rider has to adhere to when trotting over cavalletti are as follows:

1. Ride straight.
2. Quiet but not inactive pace.
3. Low neck position with a light contact and low hands.
4. Follow the movements preferably in rising trot.

Special attention should be given to an active stride. The reins should rather be a bit too long so that the horse does not feel at all restricted. Trying to force the horse into a special outline is only asking for resistance and restlessness. Frequent patting on the neck pleases and relaxes the horse. We can use the cavalletti to improve the trot as we did with the walk. To do this we gradually increase the distances from 1·30 m to 1·50 m. The rider does rising trot and has a light contact with the horse's mouth. A few lengths before the cavalletti he increases the driving aids to ask for a lengthened trot. It is important that the activity is gradually increased on approaching the cavalletti as the best lengthening can be achieved in this way. If it is too free too early, there is a danger of "running"! The horse tenses up, canters or loses its rhythm in the approach. The exercise of "lengthened trot" over cavalletti needs careful attention to the tempo. The rider gets a feeling for the horse's length of stride, knows when it is correct and gets his eye in for the right distance. In that way this exercise will be a help when jumping and riding across country.

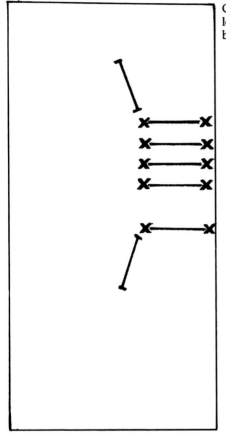

Cavalleti positioned for no strides followed or preceded by two with one stride between

An exercise to make the horse attentive is trotting over cavalletti with a stride in between. One removes one of the cavalletti in the middle of the row, so that there is a void and the horse has to trot one step without the cavalletti. This will make it pay attention and will be of help when it has to go over uneven ground. The distance for working trot is 1·30 m. The job of the rider is to achieve an even trot over the cavalletti by sufficient driving aids. The trot step without the cavalletti must not be shorter or the horse will lose its rhythm and stumble. I do not think it is a good idea to increase the height to 35 cm as the horse will become suspicious and think one is trying to trip it up. Jumpers in particular get worried, as they are often asked to jump over fences at wrong distances to make them more careful before going into the ring.

The best time for these exercises is in the middle of a lesson. Trotting over cavalletti can be combined with work on the circle. In my experience it is best to put three cavalletti on a circle. There are, of course, all sorts of alternatives which I have described in my book *Cavalletti*. There is no limit to the variations and it is up to the trainer to decide which is most suitable for his work and final aim.

115

We must be quite clear in our minds that riding over cavalletti on a circle makes great demands on the horse's physique. The inside hind leg works especially hard and can be damaged by working too long and perhaps incorrectly. The rider should make quite certain that the horse has reached the stage where it can do this work without trouble. It is only ready when it can trot happily and safely over cavalletti in a straight line. Only then should it be asked to trot over them on a circle and one must be careful to ride in the centre of the cavalletti. "Enlarging the circle" demands obedience as well as lengthening of stride and more weight on the inside hind leg. The limit is nearly reached in this exercise and it is easy to ask for too much. It should only be ridden a few times on each rein.

CAVALLETTI WORK IN CANTER   Riding over cavalletti at the canter simply is jumping over low obstacles which are spaced out over specific distances. The jump over an obstacle is a lengthened and heightened canter stride.

It is, therefore, obvious that cantering over cavalletti is of special use for jumpers and eventers. This has to be taken into consideration when putting up cavalletti. The height of 50 cm is the best in my experience. The horse pays little attention to anything lower. The canter stride stays flat and goes forward. The horse just goes faster and gets stronger instead of more attentive and settled, so that nothing of value is achieved. But when cavalletti are at 0·50 cm the horse has to jump. It is therefore enough when only three cavalletti are used. The distance should be 3·50 m. The distance, of course, depends on the size and stride of the horse. The value of cavalletti work at the canter is too small for dressage horses and not worth the effort. It might be thought that this work would lead to a better canter stride but it does not. The dressage canter demands an up and forward movement of the fore hand and the hind legs coming under the horse with a lowered croup.

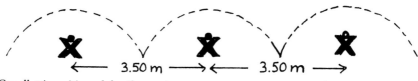

Cavalletti positioned for the canter

When jumping over cavalletti the hind legs are also pushed up. The canter movement therefore is different from the one that is asked for by the dressage rider. It is enough to trot and walk over cavalletti and no need to canter.

Cavalletti are useful for the education of the jumper and eventer as they demand confidence, strength and agility and should be started over just one cavalletti followed by a small jump. I will go further into this in the next chapter. To jump several cavalletti demands the so-called "Bounce jump" without a stride in between.

14 Jumping

The initial jump training consists of basic gymnastic training. Even the layman understands that repeated jumping over the same fences gets monotonous and it does not improve the jumping technique either, as too much is left to chance. There are critics who say that horses are cowards and would not jump of their own free will. I do not share this view, but as in the other disciplines, there are talented and not so talented horses. It is impossible to make a jumper using force. There may be initial success when rough methods are used but it does not last, experience has shown this.

To make a horse a successful jumper, systematic training has to be followed. The basic training is a necessity. The first task is to make the horse enjoy jumping and keep it doing so. Also to make the horse understand that there is nothing to be frightened of nor that it is impossible to get over obstacles. When we have achieved this we start teaching the right approach to jumping. A horse that can jump a small course with confidence and pleasure has had the right preparation to become a showjumper. Sadly, often not enough attention is paid to the basic training.

Loose jumping

Loose jumping is part of the basic training of a young horse. The value as such to training the horse to jump is small but for loosening up the horse and watching its natural approach to jumping gives us useful hints as to its ability. That is why horses are loose jumped at élite auction sales.

Horses are loose jumped regularly once a week at the leading training establishments in Germany. Even dressage stables make use of it. Otto Lorke, who was one of the most successful trainers of dressage horses before and after the Second World War, used this method. The procedure is to place two inviting jumps along the long side at a distance of 10·50 m. Wings are put on the inside to reduce the chance of the horse running out. One person stands at the end of the long side with a rope, accompanied by another who will catch the horse. At each jump someone stands with a whip for use if the horse should hesitate. The most important thing is that the young horse should enjoy the jumping, lose all inhibitions and let himself go. The trainer has to have a real feel for this.

The horse is led at the walk towards the jumping lane. Often horses are hesitant when first confronting a jump, but this is only a sign of caution. When the second attempt is made the trainer with the whip has to watch whether the horse pulls on his own or needs to be driven. Most mistakes are made by a too vigorous use of the whip. Cracking the whip and shouting are poison to the young horse's nerves. The people helping the trainer must stay quiet and give the horse the necessary confidence, otherwise loose jumping only creates problems. The secret of success is letting the horse work on its own and in this way it learns to place itself.

The jumps should be inviting and encourage the horse to jump them happily and relaxed. I recommend that a cavalletti is used as a first jump at the maximum height of 50 cm, to make it easy for the horse, and the second jump a spread which can be gradually heightened and widened. As a rule, the horse should jump these obstacles three to four times and always finish on a good note. If this does not happen the jump should be lowered so that the horse will go back happily to the stable.

Loose jumping can always be practised on the lunge. Personally, I have not often tried this. I prefer to loose jump the horse in the school as there is

Position of obstacles for loose jumping

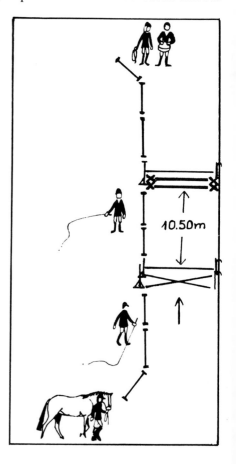

10.50m

Loose jumping. An impressive high jump in exemplary style over a spread fence

less pressure on the horse. When jumping them on the lunge one has to be constantly on the lookout not to catch the lunge rein on the jump. It is also more difficult for the horse to jump on the circle as it changes leg and so is in canter on landing. I will not deny that at shows one can see people lungeing their horses over jumps, but these are usually experienced horses. For basic training I prefer to loose jump the young horse.

Jumping with a rider

We have now prepared the young horse with cavalletti work and loose jumping. A further good exercise is to trot the horse over poles and odd small fences scattered about the school. In this way the horse will get used to coloured objects and not worry about them. In my experience a horse that has had such a varied education is less likely to shy at the like of the judges box, flowers and so on.

JUMPING OVER SINGLE FENCES   As soon as the horse has learned to move with rhythm and "losgelassen" under the rider, trots happily over   119 cavalletti and small jumps, we can progress to the next stage in our horse's education which consists of practicing the right approach to jumping. The fences are raised from 50 cm to 80 cm and have wings to prevent running out. The rider proceeds in trot, takes hold of the neck strap and lets the reins slip through his hands. Most horses gather momentum when approaching a jump. The less the rider interferes with the horse the better, he only has to concentrate on staying with the horse's movement. Under no circumstances must he be left behind and perhaps over pull on the reins. The pain this could cause a young horse can put him off jumping for a long time. It is important to ride straight on after landing until the horse comes back to trot, encouraged to do this by the use of voice. We try to get the horse to jump from the trot as it is easier for him to judge when to take off. We should not pull it back if it starts to canter a few strides before the jump provided it is not going too fast. The rider should not use force to restrain the horse before the jump. It is better to shorten the approach possibly out of a turn. It also helps not to keep on going over the same fence but to vary them. For a young horse it is enough to jump four to six jumps from the trot about twice a week. More should not be asked at this stage of their education. Several difficulties are bound to crop up when one is beginning to jump over single fences and the rider has to be prepared for these.

What do I do when the horse runs out? Most horses run out to the left as the turn to the left is easier for them. If the young horse looks as though it wants to run out it is best to have a lead horse. As soon as the rider feels to which side the horse wants to run out, he eases the rein on that side and takes a stronger contact with the opposite rein. The legs keep urging the horse forward. Should the horse then run out, it must be brought to a halt straight away. A turn on the fore hand is then made in the opposite direction to the one the horse was running out from and, returning to the start, another turn on the fore hand is made before starting the exercise again. The rider should then be more prepared and takes a stronger contact on the opposite side to the one in the direction the horse wants to run out and eases the rein on that side. If the horse keeps running out to one side that is a sign that its natural crookedness has not been eradicated. The best thing to do then is to go back to the exercises for straightening the horse before continuing with the jumping.

What do I do when the horse gets strong and pulls? This, as such, is a natural reaction. When the horse has got used to the small coloured fences and is confident it will try to get over the obstacles as quickly as possible. This applies especially to thoroughbreds and horses with a lot of thorough-bred blood in them. I settle them by riding round the jump quite a few times on both reins to take their mind off the actual purpose of the exercise. Careful work over cavalletti and gymnastics, as explained in earlier chapters, will help us here, but not least of all plenty of patience.

What do I do when the horse does not pull on approaching the jump? Not all horses are forward thinking and keen to go. This is especially evident with geldings when they are 3 to 4-year-old. I recommend taking them out for a hack in company with other horses. This often makes them wake up. It does not necessarily mean that a horse is lazy because it occasionally refuses. We sometimes have to ask ourselves whether the horse understands these new lessons. If a lead horse is available it should be used a few times to help the youngster. Excessive driving on should only be used in very exceptional circumstances. The horse should learn to work on its own and thoroughly develop the correct way to jump.

GYMNASTIC JUMPING As the education has reached the point where the horse is obedient to the aids, gymnastic jumping can now be introduced to improve its style and to supple it. By gymnastic jumping we mean putting up a combination of cavalletti with a fence at the end.

The cavalletti is 50 cm high with a distance of about 5·50 m to the jump, the height being 80 cm to 1 m at the beginning. The exercise is ridden so that the rider approaches at the trot, takes the first canter stride over the cavalletti and canters on over the poles. The combination is built to be ridden like this.

The approach at the trot helps to settle the horse. The height of 50 cm is especially chosen to make the horse canter over the cavalletti and not trot, as the distance is only right if he jumps over the cavalletti and does not trot to meet the next jump correctly. If the rider did not want to canter over the cavalletti, the distance would have to be either 3·50 m or 7 m as one reckons that one canter stride is 3·50 m.

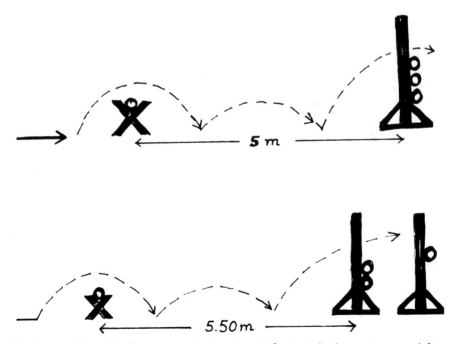

Positions of obstacles for gymnastic jumping at the trot: (*top*) 5 m to an upright; (*bottom*) 5·50 m to a spread

The fence itself should be as inviting as possible at the beginning. A small spread with a lower front pole would be most suitable. The distances should be changed as the jump develops. The distances for uprights should be shortened to 5 m. For an oxer or spread it should be 5·50–6 m.

The main aim of gymnastic jumping is to give the horse confidence in its ability. The rider has to place the horse correctly every time when jumping single fences. If he makes mistakes the horse can lose its confidence, especially over bigger fences. The only thing the rider has to do is to not let the horse canter before reaching the cavalletti. Even so, there are several typical mistakes which are to be avoided. The worst mistake is to canter approaching the cavalletti when the distance is set for trot. The horse has to accept the rider's aids willingly and trot when asked. It is, therefore, important to work the horse thoroughly before jumping.

Strong horses need longer preparation before the jumping can begin. It is best to turn them out of a volte two to three horselength distances from the cavalletti. The rider uses working trot and rises. If sitting trot is used there is the danger that the rider might be left behind the movement and not be able to go with the horse over the jump. Anyway, the approach should be lively so that the rider does not have to push too much between cavalletti and fence as this could make him come behind the movement. A balanced jumping seat is very important.

When the horse has jumped correctly two or three times, the fence can

Gymnastic jumping over a cavalletti and a small spread. The approach is made in trot and the horse is attentive and jumps the cavalletti in good style. Over the fence the reins are a little tight and the hands of the rider should be more in the direction of the horse's mouth. Erdmuthe Rosner on "Feuerball"

then be raised and widened. To widen it, the pole at the back is moved out so that the distance from the cavalletti remains the same.

Each lesson must have a special aim, to practise either uprights or spreads. Some horses tend to get too close and take-off under the fence, so they have to be schooled over spreads. Others take-off too soon and have difficulties in lifting themselves. For these it is best to shorten the distances.

Those people who want to try out the horse over jumps can use gymnastic jumping without any qualms, as it makes it easy for the horse to arrive at the correct take-off point. No more than 10 to 15 exercises should be asked for at one time so that the horse's strength is not over taxed.

To finish up I think it is good to take away the cavalletti and jump the fence on its own a few times. The result should show what horse and rider have learned from the previous exercises. The cavalletti and fences can be put up in all sorts of variations to carry on with the schooling for jumping. To school the horse to jump doubles and trebles all that has to be done is to put additional fences following the original fence. For example, at 7 m, 10·50 m, 14 m distance and so on. In this way the young horse gets used to jumping combinations without getting unnecessarily worried about it.

COMBINATION OF SEVERAL CAVALLETTI FOR GYMNASTIC JUMPING
If horses are apt to rush fences and want to canter over cavalletti a useful tip is to put up several cavalletti in front of the fence About four cavalletti are put

Gymnastic exercises at the
trot for a horse which rushes

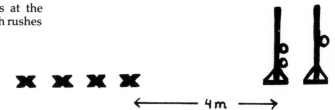

up at their lowest height of 15 cm to 20 cm to trot over and are followed by the fence at 4 m distance.

This exercise is different from the basic one as the horse is asked to trot over the cavalletti and it is left to him to decide whether he trots or canters over the fence. This is ridden in rising trot. The short distances between the cavalletti, about 1·30 m, should encourage the horse to trot over the cavalletti. The fence should not be high as the horse has not got enough impetus. If more height is asked for only one cavalletti should be used. The use of several cavalletti is only recommended when the horse needs to be settled and/or round his back more. Otherwise I think it is better to use only one cavalletti in front of the jump. To help horses that are apt to rush off after jumping, one puts a second or even third cavalletti behind the jump at a distance of about 3·50 m, 7 m or 10·50 m. The attention of the horse will be focussed on the cavalletti. Even when jumping the horse will look down at the cavalletti in front of it and will also unconsciously round its back. It will not have time to run off and the rider can keep control. If the horse still keeps

Gymnastic jumping which includes several cavalletti. The horse is attentive when trotting over the cavalletti and is already looking at the fence. Over the fence the horse's front legs are well folded and its back rounded. The rider's body is too far forward

rushing off it is best to ride a large volte after the last cavalletti until the horse settles. The rider then goes back to trot and either walks the horse a little or starts a new exercise.

To achieve the greatest success, it is best to change the jumps as much as possible during the lesson. Every change makes the horse more attentive, teaches it in time to look after itself and furthers the competence of horse and rider. It is essential to have a helper who can move the jumps quickly and without fuss. One should not hesitate to ask the helper frequently, even if he is not a qualified teacher, how the horse has jumped, what the seat of the rider was like and so on. This applies especially to riders who ride on their own and do not have a permanent instructor.

The practise session should not be longer than it takes to jump 10 to 15 combinations. To finish up, take away the cavalletti and jump the fence on its own two or three times to see whether the horse is quiet now and accepts the jump without hotting up. Praise the horse and walk it until it is dry. If not successful, stop jumping, go to the dressage arena and work on transitions and half-halts to achieve the "durchlassigkeit". Then go back and jump one or two more fences but be ready to compromise so that the lesson can finish without a fight.

In the evening we go over the lesson in our thoughts and try and work out what went wrong and plan a new programme for the following day. It sometimes takes days or even weeks before the young horse understands that it should go quietly over the jumps at an even tempo.

Gymnastic jumping can be of great help to us in this respect though it

must be understood that it is only an aid and only as good as the rider can make use of it and apply it with patience. These are only my recommendations which I have tried and found helpful.

JUMPING A COURSE   The aim of the basic training is for the horse to be able to jump a course of fences. It should be able to do this with confidence and dexterity as well as strength and steadiness. Only its performance over a course will give the answer to the question: has the preparation been correct? When the young horse has been introduced to different fences, jumps single and combination fences at an even tempo and with confidence, it is ready to jump a course.

It is of great importance that a good course has been put up. We have to consider the horse's degree of education not its possible ability.

The same applies to course builders at a show. A well-built course should improve the horse's performance. There are five points which are important when building a course.

1. The correct lines.
2. The correct arrangements of the jump.
3. Well and correctly built jumps.
4. The correct distances between jumps.
5. The height of the jumps.

The line taken should be such that the horse can canter on without twists and turns from beginning to end. It is, therefore, wrong to put sharp turns into the course, especially just on the landing side of the jump, unless they are really necessary. A course should flow.

The jump should start off low and gradually increase in height. The first jump should be inviting and a pleasure for the horse to jump. The second jump should also be relatively easy, to get the horse going. The third and fourth jump could be a double. The rest of the jumps should vary between uprights and spreads and gradually increase in height and difficulty.

When building a course, care should be taken to ensure that the jumps are fair and inviting. The poles and other material should be solid so that the horse will take them seriously. No big gaps should appear between the poles and no thin poles should be used. Each fence should be solid and demand respect. The back pole of the oxer should be a little higher than the front one so that the horse can see it. Poles over hedges should be bright coloured to show up otherwise the horse will be tempted to let its hind legs drag through them. The poles and planks should be securely in the cups. More than a slight touch should be needed to dislodge them. The most important points are to have the distances right between single fences as well as doubles and trebles and to have long approaches to the fences.

All fences should be placed so that they can be jumped at a steady canter. The shortest distance in a double is 7 m. Any shorter distance would require acrobatics. When building a double of a spread and upright, attention should be paid to the flatter landing after the spread. The best distances for this are 7·50 m to 8 m and 15 m if three canter strides in between are

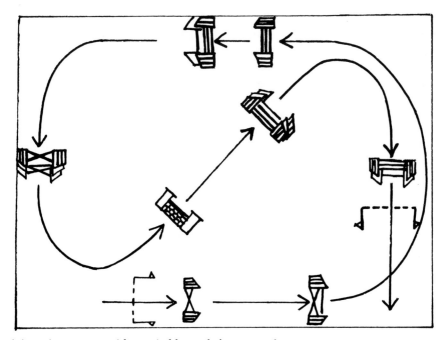

A jumping course with a suitable track for young horses

asked for. The height of the fences depends on the class which is being jumped.

Riding-in beforehand is very important. Only a properly prepared horse can give of its best. And that is our aim. We should spend about 30 minutes before jumping a course.

When we school our horse the jumping always comes at the end of the lesson. So now we start off with loosening up exercises, continue with the exercises for "durchlassigkeit" and make a few practise jumps. It is good for the young horse if we use some of the jumps on the course for this. In the second year of their education we choose different fences to jump over for practise jumps, as when it comes to jumping at a show the jumps cannot be shown to the horse before partaking in a competition. Three to five practise jumps should be sufficient. It is best to jump them just before going into the ring. Lazy horses are jumped over spreads, excitable horses over uprights with perhaps a cavalletti in front, the average horse one or two spreads and if it jumps well finish off with one or two uprights.

We are jumping the course as part of our work. We are not at a show but want to teach the horse to jump several fences in balance. The rider must have the horse between hands and legs after each jump and, if necessary, miss out a jump or change the sequence if the horse is not on the aids. It is noticeable that in the course of jumping the horse may go faster and faster because it becomes excited and starts to make careless mistakes. Pulling the horse back sharply will hardly correct this, as it will only create more resistance against the rider's hands and make the horse even stronger. The best thing to do is to ride a large circle round the jump and miss some others out until the horse is back in balance and cantering quietly. We then carry on with the course. We are aiming at a round in good style when we ride a practice course. We try to keep to a steady pace and avoid too strong aids. The horse will thank you and enjoy its exercise. A better gift cannot be passed between horse and rider.

15 Hacking Out

The basic training should be as varied as possible. This has already been discussed in the chapter on the construction of the lessons. Apart from that we must make sure that our horse gets enough exercise. If possible, it is best for the young horse to be turned out for a few hours in the afternoon having worked in the morning. It will do the horse good, both physically and mentally. If the horse is stabled in a town this remains a wishful dream and we have to think of other ways to give the young horse the exercise it needs. Hacking out is a suitable alternative and an indispensable part of the basic training. Weather and ground conditions permitting we should ride outside as much as possible. If there is no suitable hacking in the vicinity of the stables it would be worth while to get together with some friends at the weekend, box up the horses and take them to some good hacking country. The ride should be limited to much walking, a quiet trot and canter. The gradual building up of a young horse's muscles is an important aspect of the basic training. When this is done correctly the horse can work at greater speeds without damage to itself.

The possibilities for gymnastic exercises when hacking out are numerous. We need only to recognise and use them. We can achieve the "losgelassenheit" of the young horse when hacking out by walking for 30 minutes, first with a long rein and when possible with a loose rein. We can develop the horse's muscles and make it stronger and healthier by carefully dividing our ride into walk, trot and canter. By using uneven territory and hills we can improve the horse's agility and sureness of foot. Riding out in the country contributes to the making of a more obedient and agile horse. One thing we have to remember – it is easier to overtax the horse's strength when riding out in company of several horses. They excite each other and it is therefore more difficult to realise when they are tired. Special attention should be paid to this.

Riding-out in company

It is acceptable to go out alone for a quiet hack. However, in Germany we observed a rule at the Westfalischen Reit-und Fahrschule – never go out alone when you want to jump. An accident could happen all too easily. A rider falls and perhaps is hurt and the horse runs away. One never wishes for such a situation to occur, but when there are two or more riders one can always go for help.

Quite apart from this, we know that horses like to have company. We can make it easier for ourselves when several are together, for example, when jumping, a young horse will follow the example of an older and more experienced horse. The older horse leads and jumps first. The rider on the young horse follows at a distance of a few lengths. The young horse will realise how easy it is. I have often had experience with young horses refusing steadfastly to go over a water jump. If an experienced horse jumps in front a young horse will follow without hesitation. Here horses are seen to react like people and follow a pattern or good example. It is easier for us to teach the young horse with the help of an older and experienced one.

A group of up to four riders and horses is best when teaching a young horse. If the group is larger there is a chance that they will get in each others way. My experience is too that discipline and the necessary serious application is apt to slip a bit in these circumstances. Although we do not want to spoil the fun the rider is having, he must not forget his responsibility to the young horse. Therefore he must not just mess about and gallop at high speed but concentrate on the gymnastic education of the horse that has been put in his care. The harmony achieved between horse and rider gives a real feeling of happiness and achievement. A true horseman would have no pleasure in chasing his horse about and bringing it back to the stable tired and dripping wet.

Loosening exercises in the first six months of the basic training

When making plans for the basic training and taking into consideration the weather conditions in the winter, we should remember that hacking out should help the young horse more than anything else to achieve "losgelassenheit". How often should we hack out, and what should we practice?

As soon as the young horse has accepted the weight of the rider, we can go outside to loosen it up and dry it off, weather permitting. To dry him off outside may not be possible in autumn and winter as we must not expose a warm horse to cold draughts. When the weather is dry and cold we can loosen the horse up by walking and trotting (rising) next to or behind a lead horse outside. This can be extended to 30 minutes depending on the work we had planned for that day.

Almost any terrain is suitable for hacking. We can walk over any ground that is firm, including roads. Several well-known authors of books on eventing recommend trotting on roads to strengthen the horse's joints and tendons. I have often witnessed this in England. The horses were shod of course. When hacking out in only walk and trot there is no necessity for the young horse to be shod, providing the feet are in good condition. If we have the choice, we prefer, of course, not to have to go on too many busy roads.

At the beginning, we do not want to expose the young horse to too many strange objects that might unsettle it. The choice rather depends on the stage of the horse's education and its acceptance of the aids. Soon the young horse will get to know all the paths in the neighbourhood and go along them without question. Things that change from day to day, such as coloured objects, vehicles and puddles can unsettle a horse. The degree of nervousness depends on the temperament of the horse. There are horses that will always shy at objects on the ground and with all the patience in the world cannot be cured of this. In the course of my long riding career, I have had two such horses which I had to sell eventually as I could not get them used to flowers and letters in the dressage arena. I could only compete with them when they had been ridden-in for so long that they were tired.

A horse with a normal temperament soon gets used to new surroundings, as long as the rider is definite enough and does not get nervous himself. It is necessary for the rider to take up the reins and show the horse the object that worries it and be prepared to prevent the horse from shying away. This is one of the moments when the rider has to be thinking that fraction of a second quicker than the horse. The horse must believe that the rider is stronger than itself and that there is no need to worry about any strange objects. This will increase the horse's confidence in the rider and lessen the fright of the unknown objects.

The loosening exercises in the first year should include riding over uneven ground, stepping over small obstacles such as tree trunks etc. We should not be too fussy over what sort of ground we choose to ride. A small unevenness should be welcomed to make the horse sure footed. We must watch though that the ground is not so deep that the horse gets stuck in the mud.

Fitness training in the second six months of the basic training

As soon as winter is over and we can go outside, we can start introducing more extensive exercises into the basic training. Normally the second six months of training the 4-year-old young horse, which started work in the autumn, begins now. The education of the young horse is nearing its end. We now turn to the development of three paces, which is part of the basic dressage schooling. Getting the horse fit complements this. How do we go about this?

When horses first go out in the spring they are usually very full of themselves. They too feel that spring is in the air and want to show it. On the other hand, changes to the horse's coat are taking place at this time and it is more prone to illnesses. We have to build the horse's condition up slowly. To do this we increase the rising trot work to two sessions of 10 minutes with a walk here in between. We take longer to walk the horse dry after it has 131

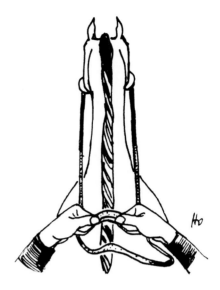

(*Opposite page*)
David Pincus on Volt, cantering in a light seat on the gallop. Expressive movement in the correct frame and with a light contact

(*Right*)
A bridge with reins

finished its work. When it is a fine day, we forget about the dressage work and just go out for a good hack. We are now ready for the first work at a hard canter.

Quiet canter work at a speed of 350 m per minute needs stamina. Short, fast sprints of up to 650 m per minute improve the breathing. To begin with we restrict ourselves to some quiet canter work about twice a week which we gradually extend to 4 to 5 km.

The stirrups are taken up about two holes to make it easier for the rider to sit forward and off the saddle. The length of the reins should be adjusted so that the hands can rest either side of the horse's mane. A bridge can then be made with the reins. It is easier for the hands to stay quiet this way.

It is best to canter or gallop the horses singly. Only lazy horses should go behind a leader but this should really be an exception. If a young horse that has been working indoors all winter does not want to gallop on, then there must be something wrong. It is either ill or extremely phlegmatic. Whichever it is, an eye should be kept on its health.

The state of going is particularly important for fast canter and gallop work. The best is a sand track. If this is not available a big level field can be used. Fast canter and gallops should only be ridden on light sand or soft grass, anything else would be too hard on the horse's legs.

Hill work

Climbing up and down hills helps develop the horse's strength and improves its suppleness and skillfulness. Include hill work in the second half year of the training, providing suitable terrain is available. The steeper the slope the more care must be taken. The most suitable slope is one of 30 to 60 degrees.

Right   Wrong

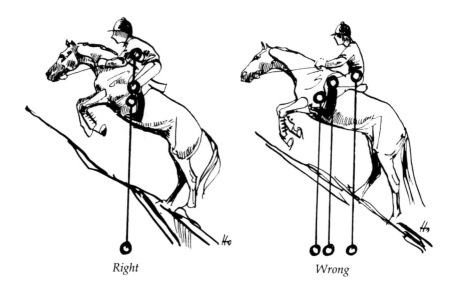

Right   Wrong

134   The right and wrong ways of going up and down hills

When we approach a hill, the young horse will increase its speed to gather momentum, but when reaching the top it will slow down as it has lost its momentum. It is the other way round when going down hill, when the natural reaction of the horse is to start off slowly and increase the speed going down. We now want to educate the horse to stay at an even tempo to prevent injury or falls.

The rider's seat is specially important when climbing. The golden rule is: uphill always leaning forward. The rider leans forward to take the weight off the horse's hind legs which have to do most of the work. If the slope gets steeper, it is best to stand up in the stirrups, lean right forward and if necessary hold onto the horse's mane. If the slope is steep and short it is best to take a run at it and if it is long it is best to go up quietly in walk. Long steep slopes are best mastered at all angles and in walk.

To go down hill at an angle is a fatal mistake. The horse loses its balance too easily and falls. That is why down hill is always ridden at slow walk and in a straight line regardless of the steepness of the slope. The rider should sit with upper body forward following the horse's movements. This makes the rider lose much of his grip so he should have his feet firmly in the stirrups and if necessary support his hands on the horse's neck. If the rider is in danger of falling off, the angle reached is too steep and the upper body has to go back a little. At a certain angle, which the rider should feel instinctively and which is at about 60 degrees, the rider's upper body has to go back so that the horse does not lose its balance and fall.

To put it concisely: uphill: upper body forward. If the slope is long, ride at a slant. Downhill: upper body forward; but at an angle of more than 60 degrees upper body back. Always ride straight down, never at a slant.

It is very important never to throw the reins away but keep a contact without interfering with the horse and always be ready to give. After each exercise, one rides with loose reins for a short break. Riding up and down hill should not be repeated too often as it is quite a strain on the horse.

Practise over typical cross-country fences

We have now got the young horse used to all sorts of obstacles by taking him out on different types of going, as well as up and down hill. At the same time the horse has got used to natural obstacles experienced when out hunting and going across country. These include ditches, water, drops as well as Irish banks. They all need a special jumping technique which, once mastered, will give the young horse the necessary confidence in its own ability.

Ditches are one of the most frequently encountered obstacles. We must give the young horse the opportunity to jump as many, and as varied in type, as possible so that it will be full of confidence and not worry when it has to tackle a really large one.

We must realise that almost any horse can jump 4 m to 6 m with ease. However, the horse's difficulty in jumping over ditches is the appearance,

Jumping an oxer on flat ground. Good weight distribution of the rider in accord with the horse's centre of gravity. The rider has a supple seat which is only a little out of the saddle. The leg position is excellent and the horse jumps with great confidence. Horse and rider land in perfect balance. Horst Karsten on "Stromer", a Holsteiner grey gelding

not the width. Once they have got over the initial fear there is no more problem. That is why it should be made easy to begin with.

We start off with quite a simple task. The most suitable to begin with is a dry ditch 1 m to 1·50 m wide. It should be deep enough so that the horse has to jump over it to get to the other side.

There are two ways to get a young horse acquainted with ditches, which will depend on the availability of a lead horse. The easiest way is to follow a leader. I trot one to two lengths behind the lead horse and I am ready to urge my horse on should it hesitate. If there is no lead horse available I walk the horse up to the ditch, let it stretch its neck and investigate the ditch. If the horse stands quietly in front of the ditch, there is no need to worry as it can easily jump 2 m from a standstill. The most important thing is that the rider himself is determined to get over the ditch and transmits this determination to the horse. In my experience most horses decide to jump after a short hesitation. The rider must be prepared for this and have his hands in the mane or neck strap so that he does not get behind the movement and jerk the horse in the mouth. If, after some hesitation, the horse still does not want to jump the rider resorts to the whip and uses it behind the horse's leg. A lot of kicking with the rider's legs often has the opposite effect. The horse just gives up and may take a permanent dislike to ditches. That is why the rider must never lose his patience. He must take especial care that the horse does not step sideways or back.

Patience pays off as I once discovered with one of my own young horses. I let it stand for 5 minutes in front of a ditch, then urged it on again, and suddenly it jumped. The spell was broken. I made a great fuss of the horse, turned round and jumped back over the ditch. I chose the same spot the next day until the horse pulled on by itself. Only then did I start to ride over ditches at the trot and a few weeks later at the canter.

It is best to practise jumping over ditches from walk and trot as it is easier

to control the horse and find the right take-off point. Later on, when the horse has got used to ditches and is obedient to the rider's aids, ditches and ditches with water can be jumped from the canter. More can then be asked. The necessary basis has been laid.

A more advanced jumping technique is needed to jump drops, jumps into water and banks. Why is this? The landings after drop fences are naturally very steep. Added to this, ground conditions are often very rough. Also water acts as a brake when the horse jumps into it and thereby slows down its movement. To counteract this the rider has to support the horse accordingly. The secret of success is that the rider co-ordinates his centre of gravity with that of the horse in the three main phases of the jump: at take-off, suspension and landing. The following study of the seat might clarify this:

a) Even during an ordinary jump on level ground the rider's upper body is further forward while in the air than on landing. The horse's back is much more at an angle on landing than during the jump from which we can deduce that the steeper the angle of landing, the more the rider has to stay in the saddle and thereby keep his weight on the horse's back.

b) It follows that when jumping into water, the rider's upper body has to come back earlier to compensate for the impact of landing. It may even be advisable in a critical situation to straighten up the upper body just before landing so that the full weight of the rider is not on the horse's shoulder as this sudden extra weight could force it onto its knees. English and Irish hunting people are known to have brought this style to a fine art, which jokingly is called "Old English".

When practising over drop fences and jumps into water we naturally start off with small jumps and at a trot. To begin with it is all a question of confidence and bravery. If we manage to jump from the trot over a low pole into shallow water, we have made a good start and can develop upon this in 137

a short time with the help of the rider's correct aids and seat. It is important to remember to approach as quietly as possible and at an even pace so that there is no sudden increase of the speed.

When jumping onto a bank it is important to have plenty of impetus as the landing is higher and the horse has to push hard with his hind legs. To assist the horse the rider keeps his upper body well forward from take-off until landing. This takes the weight off the hind legs, not only on take-off but at the higher level which enables the horse to find his footing. It is usually easier to jump banks than ditches and water jumps. One only has to approach them with determination.

A jump into water. On take-off the rider's body is hardly forward. Just before landing, the rider pushes his foot strongly forward and his weight back to counteract the effect of hitting the water. A normal seat is established on landing

The whole of the summer can be used for schooling quietly over cross country jumps. Before attempting to jump the horse into water, take the trouble to find a place where the horse can just walk into shallow water. It is important that the bottom is firm. Let the horse have a drink so that it loses all dislike of water. Eventually get two helpers to hold poles whilst the horse is jumped in and out of the water. Horse and rider will soon enjoy this. We are then on the right road.

(*Opposite page*)
A jump uphill is produced through impulsion. To support the horse, the rider bends his upper body very far forward. On landing he also keeps his weight forward to take the weight off the hind legs which can then come underneath the horse's body

16 Tips for the First Show

Entering our young horse in its first competition will show us whether the basic training has been along the correct lines. Familiar surroundings at home are quite different from going to a strange place. At home the horse's attention is not distracted and it is much easier to get it to work well. Sometimes, especially in dressage, the rider has a wrong idea of his horse's capabilities though this is easier to assess in jumping and cross country. It is more difficult to evaluate in dressage. The rider and trainer have to be positive to be successful in their training. There is always the danger, of course, of thinking that the horse is going better than it actually is. The judges' opinion can give one a hard knock whether it be in showing or dressage. That is not to say that the judges are always right and objective; as we all know there is a great need for more qualified judges as well as good trainers. Even so, I think that any honest horseman will admit that at times he is apt to rate his horse's ability higher than it is, and going to a show will open one's eyes to this. We will only be successful if we recognise this fact.

We must prepare carefully for each competition if we do not want to leave success to chance. This is especially important the first few times the young horse competes. It is not used to the atmosphere of a strange show ground and a lot of strange horses, flags, loudspeakers and crowds will worry the inexperienced horse. The young horse needs about a season until it is sufficiently experienced and can produce the same work as it does at home. Even then, proper preparation is most important.

Preparations

In Germany, our show season traditionally starts in the winter at Munster. To prepare for this we have pretend shows at home. We invite friends as spectators, specify proper start times and create something of a show atmosphere.

If one has a set time for starting, one will get some idea of how much time is needed for riding-in. There are certain guidelines. A trained horse needs 30 to 45 minutes before starting a dressage test. A lazy horse needs less time, a very active horse possibly more. The preparation should be divided into loosening exercises to begin with and then riding some of the movements required in the test. This will show us which movements the horse finds difficult and which easy. Try to avoid a confrontation before the start.

There is the danger, of course, that the rider will repeat the difficult movements in the attempt to improve them. This can create problems on the day of the show. The rider runs the risk of overdoing it, getting at odds with his horse and quite likely spoiling the whole test. Here, rider and trainer have to develop real understanding. If the horse has definite difficulties with a movement the rider has to do the best he can but cannot start schooling there and then. What the horse has not learned by the time he gets to the show, he will not learn just before the start of a test. That is why a rider should pay more attention to the basic work, to the "durchlassigkeit" and calmness of the horse, before entering the arena.

To achieve this, one should select certain days when one times the preparation for a test. This will give one some idea how long is needed, 15, 30, 45 minutes or even a whole hour. My advice, based on my experiences, is not to skimp the riding-in time. Mistakes occur if the rider has not left himself enough time to ride-in. It is better to allow more time than having to rush. Every rider should make this a rule when competing.

Show atmosphere creates its own rules

One can practise "shows" at home but, of course, the atmosphere is different when it comes to the real thing; it is more exciting and unpredictable. That is the attraction of competitions. If everything could be worked out and calculated beforehand, there would be no surprises. When going to the first show, we should increase the riding-in time by 30 minutes. I have had horses that got so excited and inattentive that I had to ride them in for 2 to 3 hours before I could start. The next week at a different show the horses were quite different and only needed the normal time for riding in.

The same rules apply for the first start at a jumping show. The riding-in preparation is the same as practised at home and which I described in the chapter on jumping. In addition to this, the rider must know the course to be jumped. He must look at the plan of the jumps and then walk the course just as he will jump it – from start to finish. He will decide at each jump where to take-off and that depends on several factors: a) The direction of the approach; b) the position of the next jump; c) the condition of take-off and landing i.e. uneven ground or deep ground; d) the nature of the jump. When there is a double, one should stride it out to work out the speed at which to approach it. Experienced riders, when walking the course, will note where to turn to save the most time. When first competing we should not worry about that but aim at a good style and not the shortest time. We should not get discouraged if we are not successful straight away. Even the best riders have their bad days despite careful preparation. After all, a horse is not a machine.

Each start should make one think. It is therefore important after the show to work out what was good and what went wrong, not only the result. What matters is to get an answer to the questions asked and hints for future work.   141

Appendix

Plans for training from basics to readiness for the first competition

The following plan for training is naturally only a guideline to the time required for the horse to be ready for its first competition. The plan should give food for thought and help to keep to the guidelines. It is up to the trainer/rider to decide how much to ask of the horse, how much it is felt the horse is capable of understanding and able to follow the questions asked. It can, of course, happen that one certain phase will take longer than others. Care has to be taken when the different phases are more quickly gone through than the plan suggests. We then have to ask ourselves if our horse is really such a "super horse" that it understands and learns so quickly without damaging itself mentally and physically. It is very seldom that this is so. The sound advice of an experienced trainer is to always take all the time required and take a break now and then to go back quietly over the lessons already learned.

First month (September)

THEME Getting the horse accustomed to its stable and new surroundings and preparing it for backing. Getting used to stable and groom as well as different feeding. The horse's permanent groom gets it used to stable routine. We watch the horse when it is loose in the school. Saddle and bridle are put on during the second week. We lead the horse out for a walk, explore the neighbourhood and stable and school. Second and third week we practise leading the horse and the fourth week we can practise loose jumping for the first time.

Second month (October)

THEME Lungeing and first mounting. Lunge the horse for eight to ten days. Have it move loose in the school with side reins. Walk it quietly over cavalletti on the lunge and lead it over single coloured poles. During the second week aim at getting the horse to trot rhythmically and "losgelassen" on the lunge. The side reins are taken off when walking and leading over poles. In the third week get on for the first time. Practise getting on and off and during the third and fourth week, get the horse used to the rider's weight. Trot is always ridden rising. Loose jumping helps to vary the routine and letting it loose in the school helps it to gain balance and "losgelassenheit".

Third month (November)

THEME Development of "losgelassenheit" under the rider, and development of activity and taking the bit on the lunge. Quiet rising trot on both reins. Walk and trot over cavalletti and single poles, if possible behind a lead horse. Hacking out in the company of an older horse. Encouraging the horse to go forward on the lunge with the aid of voice and whip. Short spells of canter on the lunge. Developing the horse's activity and taking of the bit by occasionally increasing the tempo of the trot, taking great care that the reins are properly adjusted. Work over cavalletti without rider to strengthen the back muscles. Loose jumping in the school. Leading the horse in-hand.

Fourth month (December)

THEME   Obedience to forward aids. Developing "schwung" and lightness of movement under rider. Acceptance of the forward leg aids. Teaching the horse to take a light contact with the bit under the rider. Hacking out, weather permitting. Cantering with a forward seat on the gallops. Trotting over miniature obstacles either indoors or out. Repetition of the lessons learned in the third month.

Fifth month (January)

THEME   Obedience to lateral aids. First jumping lesson. Practising turns on the fore hand, leg yielding, increasing and decreasing the size of circles. Obedient halts. Further development of the horse's activity and consolidation of the taking of the bit by lengthening the stride in working trot along the long side. Repeated strike-off to the canter in the first corner of the short side and allowing it gradually go back to trot after one or two rounds.

Hacking out, weather permitting, getting the horse used to uneven ground and small ups and downs, supported by work on the lunge, and loose jumping. Cavalletti work in walk and trot. Jumping single fences from the trot. To loosen the horse have it long and low and at the end of the lesson, let it take the reins slowly out of the hands until it is on a long rein. Repetition of the exercises of the previous months.

Sixth month (February)

THEME   Riding serpentines and circles. Development of the jumping technique over single fences. When working the horse concentrate on riding correctly through corners. Ride serpentines, large circles, turns, correct shapes of the circles and figures of eight to bend the horse evenly on both sides. Ride similar movements around the jumps and now and then jump a single fence from the trot. During the second half of the month get the horse used to gymnastic jumping. On the whole repeat exercises as carried out before.

Seventh month (March)

THEME   Exercises to achieve "durchlassigkeit". Gymnastic jumping. This month establish the obedience exercises by giving and taking reins, thereby achieving the "durchlassigkeit" with the horse's action coming from behind (lengthening strides) and from fore hand to hind legs (shortening the strides and speed). Giving and taking the reins in trot on straight lines and canter mainly on the circle. Practise the rein-backs. In the third and fourth week ride through the Preliminary, or Novice tests once a week. On the whole repeat and establish the things the horse has learned in the previous months.

Improve the jumping through gymnastic exercises. At the end remove the cavalletti and go over a few fences at a canter. Ride out according to the weather.

Eighth month (April)

THEME   Improvement of the horse's straightness and "schwung". Relaxed rides in   143 the open country. Try to eliminate the horse's natural crookedness by riding "shoulder fore" and apply diagonal aids on the circle to achieve the crossing of legs to the outside. Pay special attention to the development of the three basic paces and the lengthening of the strides. In between the exercises stroke the horse's neck when trotting and cantering and at the end of the lesson let the horse stretch its neck by letting the reins be taken slowly out of the hand.

It is spring. The work outside takes predominance. Let the horse have a gallop now and then. Practise over typical and easy cross-country fences. The fresh air and freedom of the open spaces is the most important. Otherwise continue with the exercises of the previous months.

During the last weeks prepare for the first showjumping competition and jump over a combination of fences from a canter.